I0617864

THE ANGELS' GUIDE TO HAPPINESS AND PROSPERITY

The Angels' Guide To Happiness & Prosperity

Complete with Recorded Online Meditations

By
KATRINA BLECHER

BOOKS

Adelaide Books
New York / Lisbon
2022

THE ANGELS' GUIDE TO HAPPINESS AND PROSPERITY
Complete with Recorded Online Meditations
By Katrina Blecher

Copyright © by Katrina Blecher
Cover design © 2022 Adelaide Books

Published by Adelaide Books, New York / Lisbon
adelaidebooks.org
Editor-in-Chief
Stevan V. Nikolic

All rights reserved. No part of this book may be reproduced in any manner
whatsoever without written permission from the author except in the case
of brief quotations embodied in critical articles and reviews.

For any information, please address Adelaide Books
at info@adelaidebooks.org
or write to:
Adelaide Books
244 Fifth Ave. Suite D27
New York, NY, 10001

ISBN: 978-1-958419-52-6
Printed in the United States of America

To Tony.
Thank you for your love, friendship and enduring faith
and support.
I adore you and our life together.

Katrina Blecher

Contents

Introduction

The Angels' Guide to Happiness & Prosperity is an uplifting book that reveals you're never alone and always protected. Even if you don't believe in angels—or you're not sure they exist—your angels or "spirit guides" are with you: watching over you, loving you, and sending you messages you might interpret as instincts, insights, or "gut" feelings.

This book shows how you can talk with your angels to identify and overcome the negative emotions we all face. For example: illness, anxiety, loneliness, anger, grief, depression, low self-esteem, etc. Speaking with your spirit guides, however, isn't just about feeling better. It's about discovering what's causing our negative emotions, and it's about taking greater control of our thoughts and lives.

That's the true meaning of happiness and prosperity. In that sense, your angels will guide you to enlightenment. You don't need to be enlightened to have a good life; it's just impossible to have a bad life if you are enlightened (with a few exceptions, think imprisoned Tibetan monks).

No matter what your other relationships in life are like, you can rely on your relationships with your angels. Doing so will help you have better relationships with others, and yourself—which is the most important relationship you will ever have. When you meet these higher spiritual beings, you'll feel such love and companionship you'll be transformed and experience more inner peace.

If you're in a dark place and feel you don't deserve happiness and prosperity—or you think it's impossible for you to ever achieve them—this book will change your mind. We all deserve to be loved, and love ourselves completely. According to the angels, prosperity isn't just about monetary wealth. Prosperity comes in many forms, all that glitters isn't gold, and you have the means within you to manifest your needs and desires.

This book will speak to you—like your angels—whether you're completely new to self-exploration or a skilled practitioner. It talks about spirit guides in an easy-to-understand way, demystifies meditation, and explains the science behind it. And, if you're worried about what your angels might tell you, don't be. Angels are never critical; they simply provide love and—when we ask for it—answers to our questions.

In fact, this book is the result of asking my angels what I should be doing with my life. That request turned into a collection of conversations with my spirit guides that became the basis of this manuscript. This book will show you how to meet your own loving and wise spirit guides, and you can ask them any question that interests you, though I provide meditations and questions to help you get started.

This book is laid out as a practical guide similar in structure to *The Artist's Way* by Julia Cameron. I've distilled what I've learned from my angels into an easy-to-follow, step-by-step, guide. It first explains what angels are and how to meet them. Then it shares a series of steps to overcome the barriers impacting the quality of your life. There's a chapter for each important topic related to prosperity and happiness—my angels picked the topics.

They recommend you read one or two chapters a week. Within each chapter you'll discover the angels' point of view on the topic, as well as suggested exercises and guided imagery meditations. Each week, you'll find yourself overcoming or "healing" a negative issue, allowing yourself to thrive. Most of the progress will occur while you are meditating, so be sure to write down notes about what you experience. And, if you're not sure a topic is resonating with you, it could be because you don't have an issue with that topic.

I am a pragmatist and a skeptic with a degree in economics from Barnard College, Columbia University, and I spent my first career as one of the top financial services analysts in the country. I was named a Wall Street Journal All-Star Analyst and my work required travel, but I was afraid of flying. I saw a hypnotist and, after just one session, was never again afraid to fly. The mind's tremendous power amazed me, and I began a lifelong journey with meditation.

I met my first spirit guide in my early 20s. It took me a while to learn the right questions to ask, such as, "What will make me happy?" When I was a securities analyst I sometimes asked if I should change a rating on a stock or take a new job. The answer was always the same: "Those things are not important or meaningful". While I was initially frustrated with that type of response, I came to realize years later my guide was correct. So, don't expect your guide to tell you who is going to win the next Super Bowl.

Due to the pressure, long hours, and constant travel of my first career, my health deteriorated and I retired in my early 40s to start my second career as a professional patient. I experienced dozens of diseases including terminal cancer (twice), MRSA (twice), cellulitis (also terminal), multiple sclerosis (now in remission), extreme anxiety and depression (also in remission), and more.

I share this with you to let you know that you, too, can overcome challenges in your life that seem insurmountable. Using my angels' guidance, and the guidance of a skilled hypnotherapist, I've healed my body and soul of afflictions that many—including the medical establishment and excellent doctors—thought impossible. Now, with the passing of more than a decade, becoming highly skilled with meditation and communicating with my spirit guides, I'm drawn to help others do the same.

A born and bred New Yorker, I became a certified hypnotherapist in 2013 and formed Kate's Holistic Healing, Inc., a collection of some of the finest healers in NYC. I also produced a biweekly TV show for five years, during which I interviewed holistic healers about their methods and modalities. Now I invite you to join me—on the path of true prosperity and happiness—and walk with me, with angels.

How to Use this Book

There is no right or wrong way to read this book. The book is laid out with the easier meditations first. If you like, you may read this book normally, page by page. I suggest focusing on the chapters that resonate with you the greatest. To get the most out of this book, I strongly recommend that you do the meditations and exercises in each chapter. You will find the real progress will occur as a result of what you learn and the answers you receive from your angel while you are meditating.

As an experienced hypnotherapist, I, and my associates, have recorded the free, online meditations that go with many of the chapters. Links to them can be found on my website, Katrinablecher.com or Kateblecher.com. They average approximately 30 minutes each. I recommend listening to them when you can relax and have uninterrupted time. After you come out of your meditative trance, write down notes on what you learned. I recommend keeping a journal. You will genuinely enjoy re-reading it in the future.

If you are experienced in meditation and can go into a trance easily, excellent. You should go into trance and begin each session with a body scan. Then ask your spirit guide the questions provided in the meditations. I also encourage you to ask any questions that interest you or come to mind. Know they come to mind for a reason. Be patient and listen for the answer.

If you are a beginner, that's excellent as well. You are about to embark on a life-changing experience. I recommend that you get into a trance by listening to the recordings I provide. They will walk you through a body scan and introduce you to your angel. They will then ask you questions you can ask your guide. You will find that time moves differently when you are in trance. An hour in a deep trance can feel like 15 minutes.

It is important not to feel any pressure to do the exercises. When the mood strikes, when you have an hour or so to simply devote to yourself, read a chapter or two and try a meditation. The more time you spend in trance the more you will want to experience it.

Chapter 1
Angels and the Joy of Connection

"My soul is from elsewhere, I'm sure of that, and I intend to end up there." —Rumi

We are all connected. We are never alone. Every soul in the universe is united. Currently, we are having a life experience in a body residing in a three-dimensional world. We always stay connected to the other souls (our angels), but at times we might feel a false sense of separation because presently our soul is in a physical body.

Angels are all around us; they just exist in different dimensions. We all have spirit guides and we all have eternal souls. We revel in the feeling of being close to all the souls that we travel with through time. When we are not in a body, we exist in a period called lives between lives. During this time, we can be spirit guides to loved ones who are taking a bodily adventure on this planet or another.

In this book I refer to angels and spirit guides. These are higher spiritual beings. When I asked my angels what the difference was, they replied that they're just words and they differ in every language. They don't care which words we use, because they find English a very limiting way of communicating. When you go into trance and talk to your guides you will get feeling, images and sensations – not just words. You'll find it's a much more satisfying way of connecting.

Our angels are always by our side. The way to meet them is through meditation. It is beneficial if you have some experience with hypnosis or meditation. Although the terms differ slightly, I use them interchangeably. It is not hard to fathom that you can meet your angel through meditation. This is because when you meditate, you are completely focused. You have no random thoughts. All the facts, emotions and variables can enter into the analysis. Your brain takes in all the information, without focusing on the details, allowing you to examine the situation or problem, and see the best solution. Or when you meet your guides, you can ask them directly. You will find that the answers are coming from the same place.

We can find our angels when we're in a trance and will come to realize that they are there and always have been. The angels are very respectful and stand behind us. But if we meditate and are receptive to them, we will be able to communicate easily with them. They stand much closer to us then. If we don't talk to them, they don't intrude, as they are just there in case we need them.

Our angels are our soulmates. We love them and travel through time with them. Actually, we know all souls, as no soul is a stranger. We might not have communicated with every soul, but all information is out in the open and so we are familiar with every soul, even those we've only just met.

An angel's purpose is to love us and help us. In this life we are like the children of the guides. This is just one of the reasons they love us so much. They are comparable to adults around us, making sure we don't fall and hurt ourselves.

Spirit guides, and all souls, are eternal beings of light, love, music and courage. Picture this. As beings of light, they can zip around the cosmos in just a moment. This light is continually with us, though we may be unaware that it is. When we inhabit a body, our light is our aura. Science says that if we could travel at the speed of light, we would not age. On earth, light is the only thing that is not three dimensional. Rather, it is two dimensional because its length is infinite. That is why as beings of light we are able to travel and focus on souls though we are great distances apart.

Angels are also beings of love because our core is love. Our essence comprises music because all our true soul names are actually musical melodies. It is so perfect that when we speak to each other in lives between lives, we call one another by our unique melody instead of a simple name. Lastly, we are eternal beings of courage, as the Lord has seen fit to make it part of our eternal soul. Therefore, it is not necessary to feel courageous, it's just not healthy or crucial to feel fear.

So, what do angels look like? They look like us, yet different. The guides just glow so their faces shine softly like a low-wattage light bulb. Their skin is thinner than ours, allowing their inner light to show through. Angels don't need the protection of thick skin because, luckily, they don't become ill often. They look unique in terms of their features: silky long hair or none at all, very tall or somewhat short. Their eyes are quite large, their weight is perfect and they are in excellent health. Their demeanor is always cheerful as they radiate love and peace. They have a facial expression that is usually serene, but at times they just laugh. They are so wise and brilliant and always know the answers to whatever we ask. Personality-wise, they radiate love and can be surprisingly witty. In terms of dress, their floor-length robes are usually white, but their attire can also be quite colorful. We can get a sense of whether they are male or female, but they don't look masculine or feminine. This is because souls do not have a sex assigned to them, only bodies do.

The guides are quite happy, or said another way, they are always in such a high vibrational state that you crave their company. They say that when we become more evolved, we have less sadness. Why should one be so sad when the spirit guides love us? When people meet their spirit guide, they realize they are free to do whatever they want. The angels can lead them to happiness and prosperity. They find no pleasure in hurting people or doing anything negative. Their only focus is the joy in living, and the beauty of the moment.

We are constantly surrounded and protected by our angels – our well-being is in good hands and we need to trust in that. A hypnotic or meditative trance facilitates communication with our spirit guides. When we are in trance, we speak to them directly. This is why guides love meditation. We receive not only messages filled with knowledge, but we sense all the emotions, imagery, sounds and sensations they want to convey. When we are not in a trance, they send us messages that may come as feelings of intuition or instincts that help us in certain life situations.

There is no proof that angels exist. Some people do not believe in them; they think the messages we receive while in a meditative trance come from our higher selves. Others believe that the insights are a right brain/left brain phenomenon. The guides simply suggest that you go into a trance, meet them and ask if they are real. You should not feel the need to share all that you learn in trance, since you may want to keep your experiences private. Alternatively, maybe you have an exceptional group of friends who are very grounded and enlightened and will find all that you learn fascinating.

During this lifetime, we might meet people/souls that we travel with through time. When it does, we will feel instantly connected to these people, as if they are long-lost friends or relatives with whom we have had a deep, familiar lifelong relationship. You know these souls from your chosen circle. If you do a past life regression, it is not uncommon for you to find them with you in a past life.

This book reflects the wisdom of my angels on how one can find everlasting, true happiness and prosperity so that all our desires are fulfilled. Prosperity comes in many forms. The guides do not believe that money is very meaningful. Once all of our basic needs are met, we can focus on manifesting our desires and seeking enlightenment. We can be wealthy in those endeavors that truly matter. We'll have enough financial success that our basic needs are met. Meanwhile, we will have an overabundance of wealth in our health, relationships, love, happiness, and angels.

They believe prosperity is not necessarily associated with financial wealth. Prosperity simply means having everything you need. We are naturally meant to be prosperous; we just need to work on realizing it. If we are not in touch with our inner soul, we start wanting things we don't need. We might get the feeling that something is lacking and we try to fill this need with objects. But the angels say nothing is lacking. A daily exercise to remind people that prosperity and happiness is always there is to have them go into their home and look at all their possessions. People should then realize they have everything they need. When you don't feel that you need anything else, you've reached prosperity.

According to the angels, the definition of prosperity is to feel so much love in your life that you can't help but smile. The guides say to imagine everything you need spread out on a big table in front of you and then you realize it's all there for the taking. You will come to realize everything you need is already within your grasp.

For some people prosperity is correlated with happiness as they use prosperity as a measurement. But the angels say that's not correct. When we're completely happy, we realize we have everything we need. That's prosperity. People can also become financially prosperous if they are paid and use the money for what they need – and our needs are quite simple. The guides say we have way too many shoes.

Oddly enough, the guides say one way to become prosperous is to get rid of things. If we surround ourselves with our most treasured objects, we will feel more prosperous. But if we have too much of a mess and can't see those items, we can't appreciate them. They say the Japanese can be very prosperous, as their homes can be very stark and beautiful – like the beauty of the desert. They say that getting rid of extraneous things will help us find our life path as we get rid of the clutter.

People have different ideas of what happiness is. But the angels offer us concrete steps to be happy and prosperous. Some people may think a lot of money will make them happy, but that's just a ridiculously small part. It should not be associated with abundance; it's about having enough – just enough so you don't have to worry anymore. According to the guides, "if you have too much, you become obese and you die." It's not healthy to want excess. The planet, Mother Nature, provides enough for everyone so if one person takes extra, other people don't get their share.

When I asked my angels to define the characterization of prosperity, they showed me a gold mine. It was deep in the earth and very dark, damp, and ugly. They said if you want to root around in the dirt for riches, you're going to miss all the beauty in life. They say abundance is what the planet can provide, while financial prosperity is getting to the top of the mountain – that is, if you want to climb the mountain. However, there's no need to make that effort. It is not the path to happiness.

The angels say that wanting more material possessions is a way to unhappiness. It's like an amputee wanting their limb to return. The guides say it's sort of sad for people to want great wealth. We should find joy in having enough. They don't want us to feel unhappy because of what we feel is lacking. The objective is to know you have enough in your life, i.e., having the faith in yourself that you will always be able to stay warm, comfortable and have enough to eat. This will provide inner peace and self-reliance.

The angels say money brings problems. They say we only care about money because we are so young. Later on, there's no money, everybody just has what they need. Money is a human thing. It doesn't exist in lives between lives. The angels say that everyone can find prosperity in their own life. They say that prosperity can mean different things for different people. For me, it is the love I have for myself, my family, friends, spirit guides, the earth and the Lord. It's pure and simple and invaluable.

My Angels – The Book Authors

Costada

In trance, I have received names for my guides. Their names are fictitious because their true names are musical. Costada is the name of my main angel; I spoke to her for the first 25 years of meditation. She is shorter than me, just under five feet tall. She has amazingly large, beautiful green eyes. Her head is bald, she wears a white robe with a high collar and she loves me completely.

I imagine I am lying down. She always sits cross-legged to my right side and holds my hand in her hands. I ask her questions, and she answers them. The knowledge she conveys is quite different from the way my mind works. For example, I asked about food, because I wanted to lose weight. She answered that water was good for filling empty bellies when there is no food. This is not a thought I had ever had. Growing up there was always food in the kitchen. Nevertheless, she is right, as most of the beings on this planet are usually hungry. On a different occasion, I asked if she believed in God. Her response was that the only people who believe in God speak English (I am not smart enough to have come up with that brilliant a response, as each language has their own word for the Lord), and that while the concept is correct, the word is limiting. She is aware that the Lord exists.

Costada believes that people seek out their guides for answers and reassurance. They are looking to find their right path, trying to get into alignment and realize enlightenment. Costada says when people meet their angels, their whole world changes because they then know there is life after death, and they are not alone. This knowledge will provide great comfort. They will have someone who can answer all their questions. They will feel such love. That, she says, is the cure-all for everything. No matter what is wrong with us, she says we can heal it with love and that is what the guides are. They are just pure love.

Costada listed the top three questions that people typically ask their guides:

1. Are you real?

2. What happens after I die?

3. What should I be doing now in my life? What is my purpose on earth?

Costada then answered the questions quickly and succinctly.

Question 1: She is definitely real. Some people think their angels are their higher selves, but she says that is wrong. She is an individual. However, she is in a higher dimension, meaning she can just zip over to me and be with me all the time.

Question 2: People should go into trance and through hypnotic past life regression, they will see that they have lived before, and so they know they will live again. They will be amazed at the pressure that takes off their life. They will realize they can stop worrying about making mistakes. They will recognize they have all the time in the world. It will make everyone more peaceful and happier.

Question 3: Focus on all the good things in your life. Do not think about the negatives. Do not complain. Instead, give thanks. You always know that things can get worse, but you also need to know and remember that things can get better. Concentrate on your life becoming better and it will.

Arcturians

They call us "little ones." They are all very tall, about seven feet. They have long pale hair and they, too, glow like a soft light bulb. I have five Arcturian angels, yet they frequently communicate as one. I first noticed them a number of years ago. They always stood behind me in a semicircle. Over time, I would ask them to sit or stand in front of me. Now they are always standing against me in a tight circle. Three of them appear male and two female. One of the females usually holds up an oval floor mirror, so when I look at her, I see a reflection of myself. This, she says, is to demonstrate to me that I am part Arcturian.

Arcturians exist in a higher dimension than Costada, who is in a higher dimension than we are. They speak in lofty terms and are very God-like in the way they communicate. Once I was looking at some land and was considering building a house. The guides suddenly began fighting among themselves. Costada said it would make me very happy and I should go ahead and build it. The Arcturians argued with her, saying that I should not purchase the land and cut down trees to make room for a house. The Arcturians say that many baby animals would be born in those woods in the years between my cutting down the trees, destroying dens and nests, and the next buyer of the land. Costada says if I did not get the land, someone else would. They did not agree, and I did not get the land.

At a business conference, a lovely woman came up to me. She said she was an angel reader and she could see my five Arcturians guides standing against me. She said she had never seen angels that close to a person and they gave her many messages to pass on to me. She returned to me twice more to give me additional messages. It was fascinating that she could hear the messages I had heard so many times before.

Arcturians say that when a person first finds their angels, they are not sure what they will find, but when they find it, everything changes. They will feel so much love. They will start to love other people and be loved in return. Whatever is broken will be restored. Relationships will heal. Injured bodies will return to health. Their environment will be balanced. Arcturians believe that we can get to know ourselves, our guides and the

Lord through meditation. It is the closest a person can get to themselves and to God. Prayer is a form of meditation.

One of the most important points the Arcturians want people to know is that they are eternally there. They say when people meet their guides, they will see the positive in everything. They no longer will be able to see the negatives, as their eyes simply pass over anything harmful or unfavorable, and only beauty shines through. They will reach enlightenment.

John

John is another spirit guide. He appears to me in the form of a beautiful red-tailed hawk. He has talked to me for a lot longer than the Arcturians have, and years before we bought a house with three red-tailed hawks living nearby. John is incredibly wise and loving. Yet, he appears to have the soul of a bird. He often speaks about soaring in the air and riding the currents. He is quite large for a bird. When he stands next to me, he comes up to my knee. His feathers are cream and brown striped.

He normally hangs out around my feet, sometimes perching on them. He likes to watch over me while I sleep. At times, when I am in a trance, he will grab my backpack in his talons and fly me around the globe. He likes to point out the lessons we can learn from nature and animals. John says that when people meet their guide, they go on wonderful adventures. People should explore this world, and they'll see there's so much more out there than we think is possible. He shows that we can go anywhere we want while we are in a trance.

I once asked him if he was ever human. He showed me a picture of our cat, who is a dark brown tiger cat. Our cat had three small spirit guide cats behind him. They were all orange in color and slightly transparent. I asked what message they had about our cat, and was told he would come back, but as a cat. He could be a tiger, but he has the soul of a feline. So, John taught me that we don't come back as different animals, we stay as we are.

John explained that some people do not believe in meditation or just believe that they cannot be hypnotized. It's not important, he says, because the angels are still around them, taking care of them, whether they believe or not. These people think it's a good thing they can't be hypnotized because they're strong, but they're mistaken. Meditation is a gift from the Lord for all of us so that we can, among other things, communicate with higher powers. From a different perspective, people can also be afraid of what the answers will be; hence they don't want to ask. Personally, I have never known anyone who has received a critical message from a guide. The angels say we do not do anything wrong. The only exception is violence, which is the one activity angels cannot comprehend.

John says some people aren't ready to open up, but that everyone should try. There are also people who have incorrect ideas about meditation. It frightens them, as an unknown activity can be scary. It should not, as at any time you can open your eyes and come out of trance. Wonderfully, the fear goes away when people meet their guides and they realize they're not alone. Being alone is virtually everyone's main fear. But nobody is alone.

John believes that once people meet their angels, they will see they are actually receiving messages all the time. The messages can be considered small gifts sent to us by the guides to keep us safe and happy. Some people call them instincts, gut reactions or just a feeling. Go into trance and ask any question. When you are given advice, you should always follow through on it. John says to take it as divine information. There is an unlimited amount of divine information you can receive.

Chapter 2
Meeting Your Angel

"If thou follow thy star, thou canst not fail of a glorious
heaven." —Dante

*When you initially meet your angel, you will be surprised by how
familiar they seem to you. This is to be expected since you have
always known one another's eternal souls. You will also be amazed
by the intense and unconditional love you receive from this higher
being. Your world and beliefs will improve when you realize they
are always by your side.*

If you haven't met your angel yet, not to worry; you are like
most people. The way to meet your angel is through meditation.
There is nothing mystical about meditation; it is just a type of
brain wave. When we are awake and our brain is aroused and
actively engaged, we experience rapid beta brain waves. Alpha
brain waves are slower and represent non-arousal in the brain.
This occurs when we complete a task and sit down to rest. Theta
brain waves are even slower. When we concentrate or are in a
state of mental relaxation or just falling asleep or awakening,
we are in theta. We are in theta when we meditate. In this state
we are prone to a flow of ideas. Theta brain waves are said to
be associated with a sense of deep spiritual connection and

attachment to the universe. It is typically an incredibly positive, upbeat mental state. The last state occurs when we are in deep sleep and the slower delta waves take over.

Costada explains that we can go into trance naturally during the day but must be taught how to do it when we decide to do it. She says there are different levels of trance, and it is like sleeping. Sometimes we are in a light sleep, at other times it is really deep sleep. The more we spend time in a trance, the deeper we can go. However, it is not easy to do on our own. We need to have someone we trust who knows how to help us into a trance. This can be done in a group or with another person. It's more powerful in a group, according to Costada.

There are many different types of meditation. I like guided imagery meditation, where you relax and listen to the words spoken by someone, and in your mind's eye you begin a journey. Perhaps it could be something like walking down a beautiful path and coming to an object that has a message for you. All you have to do is focus on what is being said and try not to let your mind wander.

It is not always easy to meditate on your own, especially if you are a beginner. This is because you have to set the scene for yourself, think of and ask questions of your angels, all the while focusing on what is happening around you and listening for the answers. If you have meditated before and can get into a trance easily on your own, then I recommend having one or a few questions handy that you want to ask your angels when you speak to them.

Following are three methods designed to introduce you to your angels.

Method One:

The first method is to listen to a meditation recording in the privacy of your home. I have recorded meditations to go with many of the chapters. In the first meditation, I have a recording that helps ease you into a meditative trance and introduces you to your spirit guide.

Method Two:

Another popular method is attending a hypnotherapy conference. A number of speakers are there who put the audience members into a trance, and some introduce each individual to their guide. It's powerful when a room full of people meditate at the same time.

Method Three:

Seeing a certified hypnotherapist is a wonderful experience. It is very productive to book sessions with a hypnotherapist who uses the technique of past life regression therapy and can introduce you to your spirit guide. Not all hypnotherapists use these techniques, so be certain the practitioner you choose meets your goals. A hypnotherapist eases you into a trance and speaks with you. They ask you questions about how to improve a particular area of life that you can ask your angel about. You will then receive the perfect message; you can say it out loud to the hypnotherapist while you are still in trance. The hypnotherapist can keep asking questions while you listen for the answers. The ensuing conversation can be immensely insightful.

Some general advice on meditating includes that you first accept that you can go into a trance easily. Everyone can; the one caveat is that you must want to do it. Recognize that at any moment you can open your eyes and be out of trance. Second, know that your spirit guide is with you always and definitely wants to communicate with you. In addition, don't worry that you will have to go looking for your guide. The angel will simply be there.

Begin by making the space you are in as quiet as possible. Rid your surroundings of all possible distractions. Have paper or a journal and a pen handy so you can make notes when you are finished with your trance. Perhaps set some atmosphere; burning incense or candles often provides relaxing ambiance. Make the area as warm and welcoming as possible. People tend to become cool during meditation, so having a blanket handy is a good idea. Dim the lights. Get comfortable, either sitting or lying down.

The angels say that we have shutters over our eyes and that we just need to open them and our angels will be there. We make an effort to keep them out of our conscious. We just have to stop making the effort. It's a waste of energy. People have an average of three to five angels because that's just the right amount of close relationships we can have.

Body Scans

"You don't have a soul. You are a soul. You have a body."—C.S. Lewis

In this lifetime, your body is your home – you have to love your home and make it as warm and comfortable as possible.

Our bodies take care of us. We are born healers. When we are injured, our bodies know how to heal. It's important to take care of your body, but don't forget that your body, quietly and gently, takes care of you. We need to be mindful of what happens to our body and within our body and respond to what we perceive. Practicing body scans while meditating allows the body to easily communicate with the conscience mind and deepens our trance.

Arcturians

All of the guides recommend that one should always start a self-hypnosis session with a body scan. The scan will deepen your trance and let your body tell you what is wrong and what it needs to be better. Again, the only direction for successful meditation is to not let your mind wander. Meditation is an extremely focused process, and it will do wonders for your concentration abilities when you are in an awake state. Each of our recorded meditations begin with a body scan. You will be amazed at how you start to self-heal when you do regular body scans. When you do a body scan you will encounter areas that are hurting, either physically or emotionally, and wanting your attention. When you encounter such an area, ask the following questions:

1. Why is it asking for attention today?
2. What does it want you to do to feel better?
3. What message does it have for you?
4. Is there a message to prevent it from happening again?

Then give the area some loving attention. When you do a body scan, you can ask your guide what needs to be done for the area. You will receive answers. Ask what is needed to make you feel better. Frequently, the answer is to see a doctor. You can also ask the guides to place their hand on the area that hurts. Feel the hand's warmth and the energy. Notice how the area warms, relaxes, and lets the pain lessen. Feel the love from your guides. They want us to love our bodies as much as they do and treat them with the same amount of love that they do.

When you are done with the scan you should be completely relaxed and in a deeper trance. You will also have important and practical advice on how to heal yourself.

Meditation - Meeting Your Angel

[The recorded meditations for the chapters can be found on-line at katrinablecher.com or kateblecher.com. Click on The Angels Guide To Happiness & Prosperity. All the chapters will be listed. Click on Chapter 2 – Meeting Your Angel.]

Chapter 3
Past, Present and Future

"No longer forward nor behind
I look in hope or fear;
But, grateful, take the good I find,
The best of now and here."
—John Greenleaf Whittier

As you are reading this, in this moment, it's the only reality in life you have. This moment is all that counts. So, pull in all the love from the universe and bask in the present, letting the past and future drift away.

The Past

Costada

She says that living in the past is a waste of time. That is because we have been there already and we can't learn anything else from it. The only things we should keep from the past are positive memories. She says it is not difficult; we just have to allow ourselves to do it. Luckily, we have a tendency to forget the bad things. We shouldn't focus on anything unpleasant from the past because it wastes energy and accomplishes nothing of value.

Arcturians

The Arcturians explain how our past is so vast that it goes on for thousands of years. They think it's funny that we focus on just a few memories from recent years. Their advice is that we should open our mind and realize the hundreds of lives we have lived rather than focusing on just a few decades.

They suggest we do past life and life-between-life regressions and we'll be able to see how much more living we have done. We've had hundreds of mothers and fathers. What happened in this lifetime isn't that important. They say we don't always have a good perspective on what is meaningful in this life because we dwell on minor details. We have to know that one parent or sibling is just as important as all the others we've ever had. In this manner, we can take anything negative from our current life and see how minuscule it is.

John

John says the past is behind him. Why would he want to fly way back there again? Been there, done that!

The Future

Costada

Costada maintains that the future is all cloudy and there's no way to live in the future because it doesn't exist. The other dimensions contain so many other options, but the future is not one of them because it doesn't exist yet. To think about it doesn't make any sense, as thinking about it today isn't going to affect your future. Planning is okay, but it doesn't really make a difference. What's going to happen will happen.

Arcturians

They say that they don't have a future; they just have the moment. In reality, they know they're going to have more of a future and they just have faith in that. But we can't live in the future, so why spend time thinking about it.

John

He likes the future. He's curious about what will happen. He wants to see what's in front of him. He says he's not as advanced as the Arcturians because they are in a higher dimension, but that's fine.

The Present

Arcturians

This is what they've been trying to tell us to do for years. Living in the present is what we're meant to do and it's natural for us. They suggest we focus on our breathing because that always takes us back to the present.

Arcturians believe that the only way we can learn anything is in the present. There are no lessons to be learned by thinking about the past or the future. We are having this life adventure to grow and learn.

They also point out that as we age, our memories can dim. Living in the moment relieves all frustration relating to forgetting details. There's nothing to forget in the present and being in the present will help you lay down new memories.

John

The present is the best. You can feel each beat of your wings. The air just flows over your wings and feathers. It's so beautiful to experience the sensation of now. Everyone can do it – and should do it. People who are depressed or anxious are not spending enough time living in the moment.

If you want to live in the present, John suggests imagining that you are flying way up high, then going into a dive, and then falling really fast. It's all you think about. You'll be completely in the present moment.

Costada

When talking about the present in trance, everything gets all happy and bubbly, practically bursting with joy. All the knowledge inside all the bubbles is in the present, she says. Everything that exists is actually in the present and she loves it so very much. We are always and only in the present and our thoughts should be in the present with us.

She wants us to be in the present moment. She recommends the following exercise. It is preferable to do it outside while standing on the ground. Doing it with another person is such fun.

1. Close your eyes and concentrate on how many different things you can hear.

2. What can you smell?

3. How many different things can you feel and sense?

4. Open your eyes and look at all you can see.

Then tell each other what you discovered. It will provide you a lovely memory.

Meditation Exercise for Living in the Present Moment

[The recorded meditations can be found on-line at katrinablecher.com or kateblecher.com. Click on The Angels Guide To Happiness & Prosperity. Click on Chapter 3 – Living in the Present Moment.]

Chapter 4
Death and Eternity

"Ah Christ, that it were possible
or one short hour to see
the souls we loved, that they might tell us
what and where they be."
—Tennyson

As mentioned, our souls are eternal. We spend most of our time in lives between lives, periodically having a life experience in a body. Death is a very natural transition, much easier than being born. After we die, we get to have a whole new experience. We can be with loved ones in lives between lives or we can enter another body and have a new life experience. Too many people are afraid of death They don't yet understand that it's not the end of their life, it's simply a transition to our natural state.

Costada

Costada frequently answers a simple question and then expands on it, thereby enlightening us about entire concepts orbiting the question. When asked what people should do to be happy, she replied that we should dance, play and sing – and know that there is life after death. She says people will be happy to know that they're eternal, that death is not the end. It feels wonderful to realize you have an eternal soul. The feeling is powerful because it takes away the fear of death. It also makes life more fun. You don't have to worry about making mistakes in this life because you know this is only one life of many. It also removes our sadness about people who have died because we know we will be with them again.

Costada described past lives. She says people have hundreds of lives. Why? Because we like coming back. We don't come back to earth all the time. However, we can only easily remember the time we were on earth because we cannot comprehend living in different dimensions.

People will be happy, she says, when they find that by doing a lives between lives regression in trance they can remember the time they existed as souls, zipping around the cosmos, so purely happy. The problem with our bodies is that our earthly negative thoughts can bring us down. That's why it's important to focus on the happiness of our bodies, with the help of body scans, and eliminating negative thoughts because there's nothing in our eternal soul that makes us unhappy. Everyone's true core is happiness and love.

All of our relatives and friends who have died are still here and want us to remember them. Thus, she suggests we think of the people we loved who have passed on. You will be able to remember them clearly when you are in a trance. Talk to them and see if they have messages for you. You will notice that if anyone had an injury in life, they will not have it when you see them in trance. They will be perfect again. They will also have such love for you. She says that as soon as you die, they will all be waiting for you. They will tell you this in trance when you speak to them. Never forget they are still with you.

There are some people who are able to sense energy. If you have ever been in a quiet place and thought you heard a noise or saw something out of the corner of your eye, it might be a soul (a relative or friend) you know who has passed. If you experience such an event, go into a trance and ask who was trying to get your attention and what message they have for you. I have found that a common message is that they are sorry for the way they treated you when they were alive.

Costada says that after we die, we do not necessarily go to a particular place. We are beings of light, so we move around constantly, visiting with the souls in our eternal circle.

Arcturians

When our body dies, everything goes from being dark to being light. We have abundant freedom. We feel good because there is no pain. Death is actually an amazingly easy separation. You drift up and your body stays in your place of rest. Then you find yourself in a beautiful blue/white world – everybody's there, including your guides.

When we return home to this amazing blue/white world we can go anywhere we want. For fun, we can decide to zip around the cosmos. We can meet up with all the people we love. However, it can be frustrating and sad at times, they say, particularly if you try to be with a person who has a body. You may try to give them messages but they don't always hear them. That's why those who have passed on from this lifetime are happy when we go into trance and communicate with them.

When we are without a body, we can communicate with other souls just by thinking thoughts and we can understand their thoughts as well. You will notice that when you speak to your guide or other souls that have passed on and are now guides, they can communicate with you effortlessly. Strangely, when the guides speak, they don't move their mouths. As a result, instead of just receiving words from our guides, we can grasp their emotions. We can also see and hear the answers to all the questions we ask.

Existence is better when we are just souls. We no longer worry about what people think of us because everything is out in the open and everything is positive. You don't have to wonder about feelings of others because you automatically know and everyone is joyous.

The Arcturians tell us that our souls are eternal. We have been around since the beginning of time. They consider our planet to be very primitive. The reason we came to this world, or any other world, is because we require a body in order to grow. There are no challenges when we are souls so there is no ability to grow. In this lifetime we have a natural tendency to grow. We grow as we work through problems, overcome bad habits and help others. A good goal in life is to grow and be helpful.

They say that death is nothing to be afraid of and we should actually look forward to it. All the negatives fall away. They recommend seeing a reputable psychic if you want to talk to someone who has passed on. They also say that we can communicate with those who have died when we are in a trance. Although, if you go into a trance and ask your guide to help you talk to a loved one who has passed, you might find a different soul comes to you. There will be a reason for that, and it will be positive.

People decide to come to a planet and experience a life in a body. They see a mother who's pregnant and they think they can help. Maybe it's someone they knew previously. Our souls are attracted to pregnant mothers just as the mothers are attracted to souls. The soul enters the baby's body when it is already formed. If you meditate and regress to when you were in your mom's womb, you will find it very cramped. The guides say that the soul comes into the baby body at the end of the second trimester or the third trimester when there is no fear of a miscarriage.

When you enter your mother, you are no longer aware that you are connected to all the other souls. The only one you feel connected to is your mother. You don't forget everything you knew as a soul, it's just not anything you think about. The Arcturians say it's harder to be born than it is to die. They're both natural actions, but death is easier. Everyone is waiting to welcome you home and you are just so happy to be back.

After you die you may be sad to see the people you love standing around your body crying that they lost someone they love. The Arcturians, however, call this behavior silly. Then time becomes warped, because in just a moment these people too will die and be with you again. They just need to know that you're not really gone and they'll see you again.

John

There is no afterlife. There's just life.

He says there is no near-death experience. You're either okay or you die. People do come back from being dead and they describe the death experience the same way. They see the light. They see all the people waiting to welcome them back. They go above their body and they remember everything.

John says that after someone dies it's human stupidity (he doesn't mince words) to bring them back. They haven't gone anywhere; they have just transitioned. The only people who want to bring them back are the humans that are still here. He says there's nothing wrong with letting someone die. They're incredibly happy to be back in their true home.

There is a recorded meditation that goes with the next chapter on past lives. In that meditation, you will experience the death scene and what comes next.

Chapter 5
Regression and Past Lives

"All things are full of signs, and it is a wise man
who can learn about one thing from another."
—Plotinus

Regression into childhood and past lives is one of the most enlightening experiences a person can undergo. Our past helped make us who we are. We should be thankful for it. Childhood and past lives are particularly important to explore as they enable us to overcome any negative feelings or bad habits that are held over from our past. Past life regression also lets us know that we lived before and, therefore, we will live again.

Costada

One of the absolute best things we can do within the realm of meditation is hypnotic regression to help us recall events from our childhood and past lives. Our subconscious holds memories of all kinds – ordinary, good, and wonderful, as well as bad, painful, and traumatic. Costada says most of the negative emotional baggage we live with could be the result of a stressful childhood event or a holdover from a past life. Hypnotic regression is a process that allows us to get to the root cause of a problem and often helps lift the burden of emotional or physical pain. She reminds us that strong, constant physical pain commonly morphs into emotional pain.

She highly recommends regressing while in a trance to the time that could be responsible for a current distress or discomfort. Before you begin, you may feel that you have no idea what time or life in which you are going to find yourself. However, by asking your guide to take you to the period related to your current distress, it simply works. You find yourself in the relevant time.

According to Costada, our past can be likened to bricks of a building. You stack them up as you go through different lives. Some lives may not be very strong. This puts holes in our human foundation. Regression may help us find the origin of such a problem. Going back to explore and fill in the holes of the foundation can help us overcome the emotional angst in our present life. It is important to acknowledge that whatever negative has happened in the past does not have to have any holdover effects on us today. Once we recognize the problem in our past, it ceases to be an issue in the present.

Arcturians

The Arcturians explain that each past life is a step along your path. It's valuable to see where you came from so that you can see the progress you've made. You can see what's important. Money is not important, they say. You can ask your guides about your progress so far in this life, see how much you have accomplished and remember what you might have forgotten about.

The Arcturians believe that people can find happiness if they conquer their fear of death. In their view, thinking about death is number one on the list that makes people unhappy. This fear increases as we age and get closer to our own death. The guides have the ideal relationship with death. They view it as a natural transition and there is nothing negative associated with it. It is not difficult to get over the fear of death. They suggest it is one of the main reasons people should find their spirit guide and do a past life regression.

John

John says past lives are just like childhood; they always affect us. Our past is important and other previous lives are our past. John says that some past lives affect our present lives more than others. He believes those are the lives that are important to revisit.

To do a past life adventure, determine what issue you want to address and go to the life or time responsible for this trait.

Although we cannot control what happens in our past lives, it is important that we learn from them. If we have experienced pain, it is important to understand it and overcome it so it doesn't carry over to our current lives. Sometimes, that is the reason we have another life. Such past life regressions can be life changing. Especially if you live with an unreasonable fear, a past life regression might show that your current fear was the result of a past injury or death. Once you relive it, it ceases to have the same power over you and the fear is eliminated because you realize the anxiety was from the past and has no effect on your current life. See chapter on Anxiety and Rebirth, and the related regression meditation to deal with a fear.

Meditation Exercise for Past Life Regression
[Meditations can be found at katrinablecher.com]

After you come out of the meditation trance, feel how tangible that particular life was, and how familiar. You will feel great joy once you know you lived before. It will permanently change your outlook on life for the better because you will know there is life after death. Remember the way you died. Afterwards, you know you have just died, but suddenly all the knowledge you have gained comes back to you since you are no longer hindered by a physical body. You are right back with all the souls you love. Happiness envelops you after you die and you feel uplifted because you are back home in your beautiful light existence. You know the Lord exists and you can be with anyone you want just by thinking about them.

Chapter 6
Acceptance

"Beauty is a mystery. You can neither eat it nor make flannel out of it."

—David Lawrence

Acceptance is to acknowledge that everything around you is there for your well-being and comfort. You should be so happy because of that. There's no reason to fight anything. Just accept your reality with love. It's not going away.

Costada

Costada believes that things don't have to be perfect, they just have to be good. There's no point in looking for perfection because, she says, it doesn't exist in this life. One should accept reality with love. If you or someone else is sick, that's okay. It might be a challenge and sometimes difficult, but you just need to accept the illness and love them, or yourself. You also must love that part that is hurting or ill, simply because it is a part of you and you love all of yourself.

She says the best way to help make acceptance easier is not to fight it. Fighting reality is wasted energy. Do not desire for everything to be different or imagine that what you have should be better. This life experience is your current reality, and Costada says life is simply fine the way it is. She doesn't want us to be sad, so she encourages acceptance.

She admits that some people have a hard time accepting themselves. That's distressing and something that needs to be addressed. The more we can just go with the flow and accept what comes our way, the easier life will be. She suggests going into a trance and imagining that you are a little fish swimming gently downstream. You avoid the big rocks and dangers. You swim to the sunny places where there is food and you just drift, going wherever you want at your own pace. You can just accept everything and anything bad, you can just let it pass you by. Negatives may last awhile, but by not focusing on them, their impact is lessened. Eventually they will be in your past and you can forget about them. No benefit comes from dwelling on anything in the past that was negative. Just accept the present and realize the beauty in it. Know you are on your way to enlightenment.

Arcturians

The Arcturians steadfastly believe that we should just accept what comes our way and see the benefit of it, rather like looking on the bright side of life. Find joy in the moment, be accepting and don't fight it. Acceptance is the beginning of self-love. The Arcturians say that everything is constantly changing, which is the way it's supposed to be. Change is good. It's always happening. When we accept change, we benefit by the fresh energy that comes with it. Some people are afraid of change, but it is a fact of life and we must all come to terms with it. Change, like the seasons, is natural, so there is no need to be afraid. Have faith and trust that you can handle whatever comes your way.

Acceptance exists so that we don't have to fight the wrongs within us and in our lives. Instead, we just have to accept that bad things and certain wrongs are part of our own reality. Pain may come with it, but the Arcturians advise not to oppose it. Acknowledge whatever is bothering you. and accept it as a part of you. In trance, you should ask the pain why it is there and what it wants.

They say there's no such thing as perfection and that we have an annoying tendency to search for it. We often feel like we can't achieve it. However, reality as perfection is a made-up concept that is here to stay (though we might wish that it goes away). So, again, we just have to accept what we have.

The Arcturians do not like complaining. They want us to stop. Instead, they advise taking action and tell us to get rid of what is upsetting us, or if that is not possible then to not focus on it. Complaining gives whatever the problem more power. This works for anything: depression, anxiety, pain, illness or any other negative emotion or fact. It's not good or bad. It's a part of us that we must deal with. We have to focus on accepting it with love.

John

John says to hug yourself tightly and accept everything you are and everything you're made of. He offers three ideas about acceptance:

1. Birds don't find fault with themselves. Only silly humans do. If you accept the "faults" within yourself, you'll come to

realize they are just mechanisms you've developed to cope with life.

2. Look at the things in your life that you want to work on, but always remind yourself how much you have accomplished and how many more things about you and your life are wonderful.

3. Accept reality with love and see what's possible. Don't look for others to show you what can be attained. Instead, explore inside and see what's possible for you.

Exercise for Acceptance

On a page in your journal, answer the following questions:

1. What do you have?

2. What in your life makes you happy?

3. What do you want?

4. What in your life could shift and make you happier?

5. Is there something you want that you don't have?

6. Are you working on how to get it?

7. Have you made any progress?

8. How can you achieve this goal?

9. Can you accept what you have and relinquish your desire for unreasonable goals?

10. How would that make you feel?

11. Can you feel the beauty of the present moment?

12. Is there anything you would like to change in this present moment?

Keep asking yourself these questions in the coming weeks and months. When you can answer that there is nothing you would like to change, you have mastered acceptance.

Chapter 7
Animals as Teachers

"I never saw a wild thing
sorry for itself."

—David Herbert Lawrence

We're one species of animal, similar to other mammals. As much as we can learn and grow from other people, we can also learn from other animals. This is because their instincts are more in tune with their decision making, so it's important to observe and learn from their various behaviors. They have so much to offer us in terms of love, warmth, and knowledge. We're not above any other animal. All beings have their own wonderful qualities that should be appreciated.

Pets

Costada

Costada loves animals. She believes that we can learn from them, benefit from them and enjoy loving them as they can love us.

First, they provide us with warmth (I find the guides imminently practical, always dealing with survival first). It's nice to sleep next to your dog or cat, for example, because they are so warm. They like the warmth from us, too.

Second, companionship of animals is particularly important. When animals are around, we have company and are unconditionally loved. We can play with our domestic animals and enjoy their company, as they do ours. Because we are not in trance, we can touch them. But unlike our guides who communicate with us while in trance, our pets cannot talk back. An interesting thing about cats is that when you are in a trance, your brain waves are in theta. Cats are always in theta. So when you meditate, you can talk to your cat, but only if you have one.

Costada says we also benefit from simply taking care of animals. It is good to give our pets food and love and a place to live. Our souls are meant to nurture. We get a sense of power and fulfillment when we take care of another creature.

We asked Costada how a person can best find the right animal they should have in their home. Easy, she says. The animal meant to be with you will come into your circle. Some might find pleasure in going to an animal shelter to find a pet. Others may prefer a purebred animal. Whatever the choice, there will be one animal (or two) you'll feel a connection with, and you'll be inseparable.

Arcturians

According to the Arcturians, a pet is the next best thing to having a spirit guide. Pets are loving, always there and there is truly little that they do that can upset you. Pets are known just to make you feel good. The Arcturians think that pets can be better than people at times because people can bring in too much drama, but animals generally do not.

They point out that we must realize that we too are animals, and not to put ourselves above them. Instead, we should learn from them. They say God has given each animal certain knowledge and if we watch and spend time with them, we can learn a lot. The Arcturians have noticed that some people have gotten too far away from animals. Therefore, they are missing out on the lessons animals can teach us, i.e., survival, companionship, resolving differences, working as a group for a common goal, playing, resting and parenting.

John

John says that animals are better at taking care of themselves then we are of taking care of ourselves. He says we can teach animals that we can be relied upon. He feels that we surround ourselves with too many people. We should have animals around.

Wildlife - Bearing Gifts and Messages

The angels sent the following animals as examples.

The first animal was a very loving tiger with a gift in his mouth. He was gently carrying a little baby tiger. The message is that each life is so perfect when one is a baby. No matter the animal, it needs love, attention, food, and protection. It's born loving and needing love.

A gazelle was next. He was calm and sleek, and he moved so easily. His message is that we should run. All out. Use our legs. Just do it for the enjoyment of it. We don't have to go far. Imagine yourself and the gazelle running together for the joy of it.

Then there was a chimp. He's coming over to groom us. He goes through our hair, cleaning it out. He says that contact is especially important. Taking care of each other should be enjoyable. It feels good to get and to give attention.

Along came an elephant. We can mimic an elephant and walk slowly, enjoying the soft earth. He is highly intelligent and big. He grew for a long time to get to his current size, this is one reason he is so smart. He says that it is important to keep growing and we should concentrate on growing our spirit and knowledge. We should always keep growing and keep traveling on the soft earth.

A fox came next. He had a peanut in a shell. He whispers that it's the inside that's important. He says what truly matters is how we are in the world and how we affect what is around us. It's not meaningful to be upset about things that do not directly affect us. We should only pay attention to what's on the inside, which is all beautiful.

A skunk followed. He was truly magnificent with his beautiful shiny coat. In his hand he had a diamond. He whispers that what we think smells bad is our mistaken interpretation because there is nothing bad in nature. What we consider waste just goes into the earth and becomes soil and air. There really is nothing wrong, and the planet and nature smell incredibly good. Breathe in all the beauty.

A raccoon trotted up next. In his hand he had a tiny newborn baby animal. The raccoon whispered that the baby was dead. He says there is nothing to be sad about when someone dies. He said the little baby just left his body but he's not gone.

He says we shouldn't be afraid of death. He's stroking the little body with his hand. The lesson learned, he says, is that after we die our soul will still be alive and we will not be forgotten by the people we leave behind.

A white-tailed stag came out. He had a stick in his mouth. He whispered that it's especially important to be gentle with ourselves. Despite his size, he is very gentle. He says we should treat ourselves by giving and getting little kisses. Next, he took the stick and stepped on it and broke it. This is to demonstrate that it is not a good approach to be hard on things. Instead, we should be more mild-mannered and kinder. We can manifest this by walking more slowly, being more aware of where we are and being more tolerant.

Finally, a small black bear walked up. In his paw he had a pumpkin. He whispers that it has value even though it is old and decaying. He says everything has value. He's trying to get us to understand not to throw things away, but to use them. He's terribly upset about all the garbage on earth and says we are very wasteful. If we were less wasteful, we wouldn't have the need or desire for so many things. It would also decrease the amount we have to worry about. The bear says that we worry too much. He says we have to trust that we will be warm and have enough food. So, there is nothing to worry about.

While I was in a trance, I asked my cat what he wanted. He said I should place my head on his. When I came out of trance, I did and he purred for the first time. I have since repeated this head-to-head experience with a rescued fawn and a pony. Both responded lovingly, gently leaning their head against mine for many minutes. If you observe animals, you will notice that they frequently show affection with head-to-head contact.

Exercise to Connect with Animals

This should only be done with friendly, tame animals. You and the animal should both be calm, still and breathing easily.

1. Sit or stand next to an animal so that your head is at the same height as theirs.

2. Be gently present next to the animal.

3. Let the animal smell your hand.

4. Slowly, move in and place your forehead against its forehead, and just stay there.

5. You may find after a while, the animal gently leans into you.

6. Then, if you wish, put your cheek to the animal's cheek.

7. Stay still and enjoy the companionship.

8. Remember this moment. You will have a touching memory.

Meditation Exercise to Meet Your Spirit Animal

When you come out of trance, look up information on your sprit animal. See what it represents and says about you.

Chapter 8
The Virtues of Nature

"You will find more in woods than in books. Trees and stones will teach you that which you can never learn from masters."
—Saint Bernard

Nature is our mother. She is omnipresent and wants the best for us. She's there to take care of us. We're part of her and she loves us so very much. She is an excellent instructor and we should keep learning the lessons that nature has to teach us.

Costada

One day Costada said that a person needs nature in order to be happy. We should spend time outside. She suggested walking down a path we haven't been on before. This can be done by going either into nature or into a meditative trance and finding the path waiting for us. She said our week will be enhanced by the lessons of Mother Nature.

You might first find a berry or nut. The message is that virtually everything we need, we have. It's a mistake for us to want excess because everything we need is provided by nature. Costada doesn't like our desire for material objects; she thinks it's foolish. Instead, she says to spend time outdoors exploring.

Next, she showed a magazine with a multitude of advertisements all steered at trying to sell us things that we don't need. Desiring things we can't afford is the path to unhappiness. Money is the way to unhappiness. We can use a leaf for perfume.

Nature has so much to offer, and all for free. We reap the benefits of plants because they breathe out oxygen. Start watching plants. They are quite lovely; they want to keep growing and they don't require much to thrive. It's a good lesson for us. We want to keep growing, just like the plants. She says we keep growing through meditation and learning the lessons of nature and our angels.

Look at all the birds and woodland creatures around you. They are all different colors and shapes. Just like people. Costada also reminds us that we are all the same on the inside. She says there's no such thing as different races of people. We've all lived different lives and have been different races. We're all just human. Prejudice is a concept that Costada does not understand

Arcturians

The Arcturians encourage travel. They believe we are meant to explore the world around us. For instance, they point out the amazing lessons we can learn from trees. Trees are an excellent representation of freedom.

They recommend placing your hands upon a tree or hugging it while in trance. They give the following examples:

The first tree says that it is growing, and so should we. We're meant to grow and expand; we're not meant to stay stationary. We should stand barefoot upon the earth and imagine we have limbs and roots like the trees. Then, arms outstretched like tree branches, we should soak up the energy from the heavens. Next, we should focus on our feet. Imagine putting roots down into the earth and pull up all the magical energy from Mother Earth below.

We're really in a perfect place. We are firmly grounded. We can feel the energy charging through the tree, just as the trees can sense the energy flowing through us. Like the trees, we have everything we need to thrive. The second tree said it's meant to have fun. Its limbs were bent over from the animals playing on it. It told how a bear would walk over it to scratch its belly. The tree wants supports placed around it to help hold it up. Sometimes we all need a little help and support. It's okay to accept help – whether it be a brace, walker, or wheelchair, or simply a friend holding out their hand to guide you. When you have the support you need, you can keep growing.

The lesson from the third tree was about flexibility. The tree says it is very flexible and that we should be the same way as much as possible. When negative events occur, they can be like a hurricane, knocking over weak, unsuspecting structures. But a young tree can just bend in the strong winds and not break. We are really extraordinarily strong and can withstand great forces, but we shouldn't tense up and fight these forces. Rather, we should go with the flow; it's easier and we won't break.

The last message from the third tree is that we are all firmly rooted in the earth and we should never feel lost. We are meant to be attached to Mother Earth (gravity takes care of that). We are not alone, and we are always attached to, and part of, the earth.

The Arcturians emphasized that through nature we can keep growing and thriving. Know that there are seasons and they change, just like our lives change. Know that you're not stuck in any one season. Another one will come shortly. If you're in a dark place, know that the darkness is natural. It will pass. The spring will come again.

John

John is convinced that people really should hug a tree and feel its energy. It's like hugging another person (well, not exactly), but it's a totally different experience. It will open you up to a whole new way of living. The tree just needs sun, earth, and water. Nature takes care of that. It's not our worry nor our obligation. It's our gift.

Hug a tree. Feel the energy. The gentle movement inside. It's powerful, peaceful, and alive. Just like us.

He says nature provides everything we want for us to be happy and prosperous, such as waterfalls, smiles and clouds that look like little rubber duckies.

Meditation Exercise for Talking to Trees

Chapter 9
Courage

"Across the gateway of my heart,
I wrote 'No Thoroughfare'
but love came laughing by, and cried,
'I enter everywhere.'"

—Herbert Shipman

Courage is somewhat miraculous. Unlike other personality traits I refer to in this book, courage is within all living beings. The Lord has given us all courage as a gift and it is part of our eternal soul. Our other personality traits are only associated with our body in this life. However,, courage is forever with us. Consequently, our souls consist of light, love, music, and courage.

Costada

Courage is part of us. It is not necessary to feel courage, it's simply important not to feel fear. Courage is meaningful because it makes us powerful. It can show us that we have few limitations. Costada is impressed with how much courage is packed inside us.

I find it interesting that she says our smile is the proof that we are full of courage. We're naturally meant to smile, but it is fear that frequently keeps us from being happy. That's where courage comes in. Courage enables us to face our fears and get over them so that we attain happiness. With happiness comes smiling and the knowledge that your fear is gone. Smiling is our natural reaction to happiness and we should try to do things that make us smile. Keeping ourselves happy is another sign that we are on our right path. Some people, unfortunately, are unable to let their guard down. They don't know how to relax and begin to enjoy being happy. Letting your guard down is key to absorbing all the happiness that is rightfully yours. Realize you have the courage to do it.

Arcturians

The Arcturians say that we are full of courage and that there is no reason to be afraid. They encourage us to watch children and the animals as they spend most of their time happily playing and moving around without fear. Notice how they co-exist peacefully and are not afraid of each other. When animals run away out of fear, they run to safety, driven by their survival instincts. However, since we are at the top of the food chain, we have few real reasons to be afraid.

In order to stop feeling fear, it's necessary to work on finding the source of the fear. The Arcturians say it takes time to pinpoint the exact origin of each fear. But after you do, they tell us to walk through the worst-case scenario and assess the situation. Envisage yourself handling the fear and see how to overcome it. Next, determine the probability of it actually happening. Remember your natural courage and let it flow through you. This allows you to start the process of overcoming your fear.

Dangerous situations are yet another story. Naturally, danger promotes fear, but when the Arcturians speak about being afraid in hazardous predicaments, the Arcturians are very reassuring. Here is their advice. Think back during your life about all the times you were afraid. Analyze the various situations and see if there was real danger in any of them. Even go so far as to imitate the danger from which you had to protect yourself. They say that real danger doesn't happen to most people, maybe just 1% or 2% of the population. If you do encounter danger, they say that your natural courage will present itself. You should look for a way to defend yourself and attack if you must. If you are one of the few that have experienced danger before, accept the fact that it is over. You're still alive. Try to realize that just because it happened before does not mean that it will happen again. Lastly, always listen to your instincts and do not put yourself in a dangerous situation where you could be harmed.

John

Courage is something we all have, and we should all be proud of how brave we are. We should have faith that our instincts are an integral part of us and were given to us to keep us safe.

There's no reason to worry about the future because the things that might put us in danger usually take us by surprise. Examine your past and you will see the truth in this. You should then realize, there is no reason to worry or even think about the future. All those thoughts will not change the future.

Most people worry about things that don't happen. Unlike other animals, being at the top of the food chain allows us to not have to be hypervigilant of predators. Some people fear being attacked by other people. While this does occur, stay rational. Should you ever find yourself in a dangerous situation and are afraid, reach for anger instead. It is a higher vibrational emotion and will help in your approach to the situation.

If you find it difficult to pinpoint what is causing your fear or anxiety, do a past life or childhood regression to the event that caused your fear (see meditation in Chapter on Anxiety).

Exercise to Analyze Fear

In your journal, write a comprehensive list of your fears. Then, write down answers to the following questions for each:

1. What is it that actually frightens you? Be as specific and detailed as possible.

2. What is the probability of your fear happening?

3. Record when the fear began.

4. Describe what you think the cause of this fear is.

5. Develop and write a plan of action on how to protect yourself should this fear come to fruition (it's practical to plan ahead, like having fire extinguishers).

6. Finally, describe what would make you feel safer regarding each fear. This will provide a sense of control. This all ties back to patience, acceptance, faith and trust.

Chapter 10
Manifestation

"In the depth of winter, I finally learned within me lay an invincible summer."

—Albert Camus

You can have everything you want. Nothing is out of your reach. You just have to know what your goal is – and make it as specific as possible. Just acknowledge that every day you are getting closer to it because the universe will bring it to you. We have the power to make our dreams become reality.

Costada

On the topic of what we should be doing with our life right now, Costada says we should spend more time thinking about what we want to do and then do it. Setting goals leads to accomplishments, or said another way, the manifestation of our desires. This, she says, is the objective. The first step is deciding we want something and then putting out the energy that will bring it into our circle. These are actual items or actions versus perceptions. Perceptions are how we feel while manifestation is the concrete fulfillment of a desire, such as getting the love, home, or job of our dreams.

Costada says that in order to manifest what we want; we have to decide exactly what we want and be specific about it. Then know that it's going to just come to you by asking for it. Just by asking, the universe will bring it to you.

However, you have to know the right things to manifest. Don't be greedy; for example, she says, don't make winning the lottery a priority. Instead, you should seek things like happiness, health, friendship, and love. Manifestation doesn't work well for material objects because they are not important. What you ask for should be realistic. You might want to have a nice place to live, but don't feel you need a huge mansion and estate. It's not that we have to take baby steps, just realistic ones.

Costada's Exercise for Manifestation

One way in which we can manifest our desires is to make a dream board. Costada says it's the perfect way to put all our dreams and thoughts into practice. Then you must trust that everything you've put down you will eventually receive in the future. Everyone should do a dream board. Know it might take years for everything to manifest, so remember the benefits of patience.

When making a dream board you should keep in mind that it will probably take a few months to complete. A good method is to cut pictures and words out of a magazine that appeal to you. Keep piling them up. Then one day when you feel inspired, lay out all the things that interest you on a piece of paper. Attach them on the board according to your liking. She said they would be put in the right order because they have their own energy.

Lastly, consider putting a path on your dream board so you can see where you've been and where you're going.

She suggests creating a dream board every five years, since it takes a lot of effort to lay dreams out and they'll take time to manifest and become a part of our life. However, five years is just a rough outline. You might get into the flow and everything is great, and you find that you are manifesting faster. If you manifest most everything on your dream board, you should celebrate and make another one. You can certainly have more than one dream board going at a time.

It's fine to be a little unrealistic in your dream board. You can gauge it by looking back at your past. Remember the things you have wanted and then see what you have received. It will demonstrate how you have manifested in the past. Look at how far apart your desires and your reality were. This can help you determine how realistic you want your dream board to be.

So, what happens if nothing on our dream board comes true? That, Costada says, will not happen – because once we have set our mind on something, it will come to us in time. We must just make sure we're not pushing it away. We need to be open and accepting to everything. We will not know our objective is coming true until it is there. There will be a sense of excitement, when you look back at your dream board a few years later. You will feel a sense of amazement that practically everything on your dream board came true.

She says we can do anything we want. We have a lot more energy than we realize. Energy is not a matter of being physically strong. Energy allows us to come up with solutions with our guides to help ourselves. She says we have more power than we realize. We have the power of manifestation.

Arcturians

The Arcturians, who are endlessly reassuring, point out that there are signs along the way that show us if we're on the correct path to manifestation or the realization of the goals and dreams that we've set out for ourselves. They recommend looking back at your recent life and seeing the good that was there. You'll see the times you received what you've asked for and will appreciate the progress you've made.

Arcturians say we're like magnets. Once we determine what we want, the guides do everything in their power to push it towards us. But we need to be receptive. Whatever feels right, meaning happy and in alignment, is the direction we are destined to go.

They want us to feel a sense of accomplishment. This feeling comes from our mind because our bodies already know if we've accomplished something. However, our mind sometimes lags. Therefore, when our mind knows that we've accomplished something, we can feel secure that we indeed have. The sense of accomplishment comes from our core, the inside of our body. If we finish a project, we'll have a warm feeling inside; if not, we'll feel hollow. The Arcturians also say that often we have finished and accomplished things long before we think we have; we just keep going back unnecessarily. We tend to be perfectionists, but they say being just okay is good enough.

We accomplish so much in our lives and we often forget our success. That's a mistake. That's the way we should think about the past. All our accomplishments. Otherwise, it is unnecessary to dwell on the past.

If something scares you, hurts you, upsets you – anything negative – you should stop and go in the other direction. You need faith that you are able to work through anything negative and come to a happy solution. If something is upsetting you, then you are on the wrong path. You should aim to have a life where things don't trouble you. If life's occurrences are negative, just let them float on and pass you by.

If we just focus on the good events and people in our lives, life takes off. If our vibration is high and we feel as if we are in alignment, others will be attracted to our positive energy. The more we focus on the good in our lives, the faster things that we desire will come into our circle. Everything will just come to us. That's the ultimate.

The Arcturians' Exercise for Manifestation

Take a strip of paper and write a wish on it. Keep taking strips of paper and write down what you want. Next, place all the pieces of paper in a jar, envelope or bag and put it away. In about six months or a year, open it up, and you'll see that most or all of the things you wrote down that you wanted, you've attained. Then do it again, with more wishes. Some things may have come in different forms, but you will have still received your heart's desire(s). Know that just about all of them will come true eventually. It's a magical practice that works beautifully.

According to the Arcturians, people have to learn that it isn't good to dream about manifesting one thing – we should dream about many things. So, when we get most of them, we'll realize that so many dreams have been fulfilled. Focusing on one thing is limiting yourself. Don't be single-minded. You want your whole world, 360 degrees, to get better, not just one little thing.

They say that we may manifest our desires and not be aware of it. We might just feel something is better, but it's actually our dream coming true. Or we don't make enough space for it. We need to take that first little sliver of goodness and let it expand throughout our lives. Know that it's important to keep dreaming. It makes us happy and fulfills our desires.

John

John said we can be extraordinarily strong about manifesting our desires. We should just walk purposely toward what we want, knowing nothing can get in our way. Walk up and take it. We have the power. In addition, when something tells us it doesn't feel right or we don't want to do something, we should listen to that voice. Every time we focus on the negative, we move away from the fulfillment of our dreams. We shouldn't force ourselves to do things that we don't want to do. The reality is that there is nothing that has to be done that can't be done enjoyably.

John's Meditation Exercise for Manifestation

After a few months or years, notice how your dreams have moved into your existence.

All of these things are all similar – dream boards, slips of paper in an envelope, objects in a box. They help you focus on your dreams and have faith that you are going to achieve them.

We can see the truth that we have the ability to attain our desires by looking at the past, remembering what our dreams were, determining if any of them were realized and seeing that they were. The more you can look back in your past and have a positive feel about it, the more faith you can have that your future will be full of dreams come true.

If a person doesn't believe they have the ability to manifest their goals, that's fine, but he or she may not have as wonderful a life because of it. That is because part of the joy of manifestation is watching it grow and come to fruition.

Then, uncharacteristically, John was very practical in explaining how to attain our desires. He says:

1. Make a budget to better manage spending.

2. We do not need to suffer as much as we do. When something is bothering us, don't dwell on it, address it. It's important to do a good job of being aware.

3. It is good to keep active as having objectives lead to us achieving our desires as well as keeping us from being bored.

4. Remember to invite art into your life.

5. Celebrate every achievement and goal you reach with pride.

Chapter 11
Improving Relationships

"The ornament of a house is the friends who frequent it."

—Emerson

Our relationships are especially important, but they're also a given because we are already connected to one another. We should realize that we have many different relationships – with ourselves, the spirit guides, the Lord, other people, animals and even plants. It is our job to make all meaningful relationships stronger and more enjoyable. We have an unlimited amount of energy to both receive and to give. It is the loving support we all need, but sometimes forget we have.

Costada

Relationships are one of the most important aspects of our lives. Some people in our lives are critical while others are supportive, and we should focus on them one by one, individually. We should remember that relationships are not solely about us; the important thing is the interrelationships we have and the way we behave toward other people.

The most significant relationship we have is with ourselves. Once we have self-love down, the relationship with our guides is our second most important relationship. Our guides will show us how to improve relationships with our family and friends.

We need to acknowledge the truth that these relationships are more important to us than anything else: money, health, or belongings. True prosperity is found in the quality of our relationships. The further we go inside of ourselves, exploring our feelings, thoughts, and beliefs, the more connected we become to ourselves and other people.

Essential for a good relationship with yourself is that you must love yourself. Having self-love makes you feel terrific (see chapter on Love – Self-love). Your relationship with others should improve dramatically. To have self-love, learning to be honest with yourself is the key. Costada says people lie to themselves and try to convince themselves of untruths, and that's the greatest mistake one can make. You cannot lie to yourself. She says it's okay to lie to other people if the occasion warrants it, but lying to yourself will just confuse you. If you know the truth on one level and try to convince yourself of some other reality, nothing good can be accomplished.

A common lie people tell themselves is that they don't have to do the things they should. For example, people should be saving money but instead they buy something that they can't afford. Or they think they can't do something, but they really can. Also, people often feel sorry for themselves, but they should stop and realize that this only wastes energy. The angels will tell you what is important, and you will agree, since all their ideas are perfect.

Once you have completed this vital, monumental task (it's not easy) and have solidified your relationship with yourself, then it's time to get to know your guides. Angel relationships don't require any emotional work. After you are settled into a trance and meet your guide, the only feelings will be love, wonder and, surprisingly, frequent amusement. The guides are perfect because they are perfect souls. They will love you and make you feel deserving and worthy of not only their love but your own love as well.

Essential for good relationships with other people is that when you are talking to someone, really listen to what they have to say. Focus on the person in front of you (or on some phone device) and try to draw out pertinent information and emotions regarding the situation they are discussing (unless they are simply relaying a story to you about some event they experienced). If they are in a low vibrational state and feeling down, concentrate and see if the two of you can come to an enlightening insight about the issue. If you do, you will both grow, feel proud and your vibrational state will rise.

Here again, honesty comes into play with relationships. Some people are not honest with one another. According to Costada, the most common thing people are not truthful about is what they really want from another person. People also lie and complain about things that aren't really bothering them simply to get attention. Costada says this is hollow attention. If you are dealing with a problem that doesn't really exist, and you bring in someone else, this could cause damage to the relationship.

To improve relationships, Costada says to focus on quality not quantity. Quality relationships are with those people with whom we want to spend time. We really love these people and talk honestly to them. We can only have a limited number of quality relationships, so we must focus on the ones that are most important. We can't have 20+ close relationships; we can only have about 2-6 and those are the ones we should work on strengthening. We don't have to work on deciding which the most essential relationships are because we know it in our hearts. If a person has multiple relationships, Costada says that's fine also, but you can only be truly emotionally close to a small number of people.

Qualities that indicate a healthy relationship include the ability to listen to the person speaking, support (even if the person does something wrong) and love them. Being there for the other person is key; it's a two-way street. When building a relationship with someone, just keep working on the connection by talking to them and listening with understanding and intent. Eventually the bond between you will strengthen as you become closer. However, Costada warns not to lose your individuality. This can happen when some people stop putting themselves first. Then you are off your life path. Don't forget your most important relationship is with yourself.

Arcturians

The Arcturians say the best way of being a good friend is to put the other person above ourselves when the other person needs it. We should hold their hand through difficult times, and check in on them so they're not alone. Surround them with love. Give them abundant attention. It should not be any different for us. It should be equal, so that they'll be there for us when we need them. This knowledge will take away anxiety because we know we have someone in our corner.

If a relationship frequently brings us sadness, anxiety, or anger, we will know at once that the relationship is unhealthy. If we have such a relationship, the Arcturians say that the first step is to decide if we want to keep the unhealthy relationship and why. Ask yourself if the relationship, despite being unhealthy, is important for you to maintain. Ask if you can make it better and if keeping the relationship could benefit both parties.

For example, if the other person insists on taking all the attention, you'll get nowhere trying to resolve differences by having a difficult discussion. Instead, focus on the positives and strengthen them. Simply tell the person that they are doing something that's hurting you. If the person is really listening, you'll only have to say it once, and they will stop. Another example is developing a relationship. If you are trying to get closer to another individual but disagree with them about something, determine if there's any truth to the other person's view. If there isn't, you can ignore it. If there is, you can try to improve it. So, you don't have to fight back. In the end, if it will be a good relationship, the other person will feel the same way.

If people don't have any outside relationships, they should work on their relationship with themselves and their guides. The Arcturians stress the importance of having a good relationship with our spirit guides. It should be filled with love. Guides are there to help us. The Arcturians advise us to talk to our guides every day, whenever we have a couple of minutes. Ask them what we should do that day. If we can't hear them, we just have to keep asking and be patient. If we ask them, our guides will know of others with whom we can have a successful, healthy relationship.

Our guides give excellent advice on relationships since they are experts. They don't want us to be afraid and recommend opening ourselves up to one another. If you have a strong enough relationship, then the other person's intentions toward you will be good. You'll be able to appreciate the advice they give you and it won't strike you as criticism.

The Arcturians say that relationships make us more prosperous than anything else. A pile of money on the counter is not nearly as much fun as being and conversing with great friends.

Exercise on How to Prioritize Relationships

1. The angels recommend making a list in your journal of all the people in your circle.

2. Next to the names, listen to your instinct and write down whether that relationship adds or detracts to your life right now.

3. Then identify the ones you want to work on and why.

4. If there's anyone on the list who makes you uncomfortable, unhappy or has hurt you in any way, think about how you can improve the relationship, if you should forgive them or if it is better to walk away with love and remove them from your energy circle.

It's much clearer once it's in black and white (even though relationships definitely have gray areas). Also remember that just because you've had a relationship for an awfully long time doesn't mean it's good. Lastly, the Arcturians say it's always good to meet a new person. They love it when we talk to strangers.

The topic of how to deal with challenging relationships at work came up in discussion with the Arcturians. Their simple reply was, "you get paid'. That's the offset. If a troubling relationship at work interferes with getting your job done, it's a problem. They suggest pulling back from the work or colleague relationship and working on accomplishing things on your own. Don't let them make your life worse. Maybe you can't change them, but you also don't have to be close to them so it won't affect your soul.

The best way to protect yourself if someone is verbally abusing you is to walk away. If you cannot physically walk away, you can tune out and refuse to respond to their comments. They might get angrier, but you can just let their anger bounce off of you. If what they say is not true, it's just someone trying to hurt you. By loving yourself, you don't let the hurt in. If someone isn't holding up their end of a relationship, know that they will learn that lesson at some point in some life. That is the beauty of karma.

Soul mates, the Arcturians say, are the souls we travel with through eternity. We do not have many strong soul mate relationships on earth because, as the guides have said, we can only have a few really close, strong ones. Yet these are the ones that give us so much pleasure. We can identify them because these souls are the people we think about and love the most. The relationships we have with people in our family are actually ones we chose before we came into our physical bodies. So, don't forget that.

John

It's better to fly in a flock because you lift each other up.

Gift Giving

Relationships benefit from gift giving. Giving and receiving gifts in trance is one of the most enjoyable and meaningful activities in which we can engage – and it doesn't cost anything. You will be surprised by the beauty, the accuracy, and the love you experience when you give and receive each gift, in a similar manner to the gift giving in the Meeting You Angel meditation.

He believes that one of the best gifts we can give in this lifetime is to donate blood, as it will help someone else. It's a way to share our love. He also suggests sharing or leaving our organs for transplant. We will feel joy when we see how it benefits someone else when we are again a soul playing in lives between lives.

Chapter 12
Forgiveness

"If you want others to be happy, practice compassion. If you want to be happy, practice compassion."

—14th Dalai Lama

It's important to our health to forgive because if we carry around negative and angry feelings, we cannot heal. We can forgive everything especially if it's in the past because the past has no bearing on today. We can just let it go. Forgiveness makes us feel lighter and happier. Forgiveness is a gift we can give ourselves.

Costada

Dwelling in the negative energy of anger is a very harsh environment for the body. Your happiness and prosperity will increase as a result of forgiveness. Costada says the message about forgiveness is that we all came to this planet to have a life, but it's a truly short life relative to our eternal existence. We have to be kind and should not expect so much of others. She says we are all young in this life. She likens us to young children. The young don't set out to do bad things intentionally, so they don't require forgiveness. For our benefit, we should work on forgiving those who we feel wronged us.

Forgiveness is important. It is the key to peace and contentment. For example, people often hang on to anger which in turn makes them unhappy. They can hold on to it for years, resenting those who have caused them pain. It has no positive effect, but only makes us miserable. We can't be genuinely happy until we forgive the people who hurt us. We should learn to view the comments that hurt us properly, letting go of any bitterness caused. At the same time, we should understand that the people hurting us are only lashing out because of their own failings.

Forgiveness is about you, not the other person. You have to forgive for yourself. Costada says forgiveness is a gift you give yourself. Costada offered the following steps to forgiveness:

1. We can be terribly angry at someone for something they said to us. However, they may have completely forgotten what they said, because it was just a random thought that came from the child inside. People can say silly and rude things without thinking. We should just let these remarks drift away in the wind because they are not a reflection of that person's true soul.

2. When we don't ignore them, negative emotions can build and fester. Realistically, they are usually just passing comments that we take to heart unnecessarily. We shouldn't dwell on them, but instead we should think of the good times we had with the person who spoke indelicately. Wait for the person to do something good because they will.

3. If you are having a difficult time forgiving, know that any hurtful words said to you likely says more about the speaker than it does about you. People with superiority issues are often immature; they can say mean, childish things. Costada says you

also have to find out why their words are so bothersome. This is something for you to work on. Or you may realize it may be best to forgive them and move on with your life with them in a limited or nonexistent manner.

Arcturians

If we cannot find forgiveness, we should dwell on the issue and determine if the actions of this person profoundly affect our life. It may not be upsetting us as much as we think, and we could be wasting energy staying the target. If it does affect us, the problem needs to be solved. You can look to your guides for help. If the problematic person is a permanent part of your life, then it's your new reality and there's no one to be angry at. It's not right or wrong. It just is.

You should take action to forgive someone since it's to your own benefit. The Arcturians believe that fighting is not the answer. So, when you need to forgive someone in your life, do it solo without involving the other person. Focus on your own life and the people in your circle. Do what you can to make it as wonderful as possible. If someone is coming after you (to harm you) your power is taken away, and your happiness is taken away. Then it is hard to forgive but in a short while you'll be back with all the other souls, and you'll learn that it was just a small part of your existence.

Responsibility for the greater good is not our job, unless it is going to affect your life or the lives of the people in your circle. You should make your world as gentle and soft as you can for everyone. Lastly, if you don't forgive someone, you should keep your thoughts to yourself. If you talk about it, it spreads and becomes negative energy.

The Arcturians believe that everyone should be forgiven because they're just so young. If we get very old and possibly lose our memory, we again become child-like. So, we can always forgive the very young and the very old without a problem. When we're adults, we think everyone should act properly, but this is a mistake. Therefore, when adults act in ways that need to be forgiven, we should forgive them too. We should forgive everybody, no matter what their age, for our own benefit.

The guides offered three affirmations we can say to ourselves to help forgiveness:

1. God gave us forgiveness as a gift and we have an unlimited amount to spread around – Costada.

2. At the core of everybody is love – Arcturians.

3. The most important thing to forgive is ourselves – John.

We forgive others easily, but not ourselves. If we really think about it, there is nothing we have to forgive about ourselves. We may have just made mistakes, but that is a natural part of life.

Meditation Exercise to Realize Forgiveness

As you come out of trance, reflect on your feelings regarding your decision. You can always redo the meditation in the future and see if your feelings change.

Chapter 13
Judgment

"If there is anything that we wish to change in the child, we should first examine it and see whether it is not something that could better be changed in ourselves."

—Carl Jung

Judgment has negative connotations. It is also unnecessary. There are judgmental people who believe they are better than others. They can be critical, negative, and often have little respect for other people. But in this world, everyone should be equal – one and the same – thus they are wrong to behave this way. If you feel you are being judged harshly it could be taking up space that instead could be filled with joy, love, and fascinating knowledge.

Costada

Most living creatures on this planet are fighting for survival. Their attention and instincts are directed toward finding water and food, surviving the elements and procreating. Judgment is a luxury, an indulgence, something people may do just to make themselves feel better about themselves. However, when our focus is on staying alive, judgment takes a back seat. For example, if we are avoiding predators, we don't really care what others are wearing. Judgment can only exist when basic needs are filled.

She admits that some of us can be quite judgmental. We think we have so much, that we are superior, and that we can belittle, malign, or simply dismiss other people. When we have what we need, sometimes we might spend our time trying to make ourselves look good so others will admire us. Costada says it doesn't work that way. We are not admired for how we look, or what we project, but for how we act.

Costada compares judgment to the dessert. The wide-stretching expanse can surround you, yet with nothing there. It's all empty. There is no natural judgment and there should be no judgment. Judgment, she says, is having a false belief about what is important to our soul and our happiness. Every living thing is simply existing the best way it chooses to and there's no reason to judge it.

The cause of judgment is the over-inflated ego (a person's exaggerated self-esteem or self-importance). Everyone has an ego – big, medium, small, or minute – it's there. Ego is not negative; it is your self-worth. You can do things to make yourself feel better about yourself, as long as you don't think you are better than others. If you do think that then there's a good chance you have an over-inflated ego which in turns gives you a false sense of superiority. This can make you arrogant, and likely to put down others. Some people want to feel superior and this is when ego and judgment can get in the way. It's senseless to disparage or criticize others when no one is better than anyone else. We're all just living our lives.

At times, the reason that people denigrate other people is because they are scared. They attempt to deal with their fear by belittling other people, as this makes them feel better and somehow bigger. Costada says it's like a sandcastle – it has no substance. It really doesn't lift you up.

Arcturians

The Arcturians have a decidedly different view. They say that ego is something possessed by the wealthy. If you are merely trying to survive, i.e., struggling to stay healthy or make ends meet, then you are not likely to be egotistical, that is, the state of being self-centered. Ego – one that is unhealthy – is a hurdle we place in front of us. When our ego leads to arrogance, we tend to put other people down because we seem to need a great deal of admiration. We have to be out in front, a winner every time and better than everyone. But those thoughts don't need to be there. We should want to move past the exaggerated feeling of self-importance and learn to feel better and confident about ourselves. In reality, it's all about how you feel about yourself. If you are happy with yourself, it's simply love; you are not egotistical.

Some people mix up ego and self-love but they're completely different. Self-love is all positive. Those who possess self-love have the ability to be empathetic, understanding, and compassionate. Ego is self-worth but it can be over-inflated, which can lead to unnecessary judgment of others. There is nothing wrong with feeling good about yourself. When you compare and think you are better than others, then it becomes a problem.

The Arcturians offer the following advice on how to handle people with an inflated ego: When faced with someone who is judgmental, the best way to protect ourselves is to ignore them. These people do not have a well-developed sense of self-worth, but we should try not to feel sorry for them. Instead, we should try to help them by focusing on solutions and not their problems. People with large egos tend to have a hard shell around them, as they are hiding their insecurities.

Just as focusing on our best qualities is helpful when someone makes fun of us or attempts any other type of derision, the reverse can be helpful to the egotist. We can try to get them to see their positive qualities and focus on their own importance. Getting them to see that their false sense of security is not meaningful is key to helping them rid themselves of all the ideas they have about being better than anyone else. Help them to see these are false. The astute Arcturians say there are some people who may never see the truth because their excessively big egos result from insecurity, uncertainty and, at times, jealousy.

John

John says that ego and judgment are like a couple of worms. You should just swallow them and get rid of them. Spoken like a true bird. His view is that it's foolish to judge. He would rather land on someone's shoulder and poke them in the head to remove the over-inflated ego/worm. We have seen that the world endures the senseless judgment of people who criticize people due to their skin color. However, we have all been a part of different races, at one time or another. People who are not aware of this should engage in a regressive trance in order to see who they were in their past lives. When you do a past life regression in trance, look down at your feet, see if you are wearing shoes.

Notice the color of your skin and the size and shape of your feet. You will then realize you have been different races and sexes.

We should promote equality. We should be like birds. We are all unique but all the same. Everyone is equal and we are all the same underneath our skin. It's one of the great failings of mankind not to know this. The animals do. The exceptions are some male birds, fish and other animals who know that their bright colors are likely to help them attract a mate.

He says our goal should be to remove any prejudice we might have. We should make sure that we don't encourage the egotistical, prejudicial, and judgmental behavior of people we meet. Rather, we can try to help them see they are equal to all others.

Fear is the basis of this superior feeling, according to John. People who judge and have big egos often believe that someone wants to take what they have. As a defense, they try to put others down, but this doesn't protect them in any way.

If you feel you suffer from such a judgmental personality, John suggests trying to remember how accepting you were as a child or watch children playing together in the park. A child usually does not notice skin color or a particular brand of clothing; they just see a potential friend. While in a trance we can regress to our childhood and perhaps remember what we thought before we began to believe that we were better than others. That's a mistake that some adults teach children.

Arcturians on this fear:

The fear from which you need to protect your family and belongings can be real. But the approach isn't correct. If you have something of value, you should try to keep it safe, and if you have extra, you should share it. But you shouldn't be afraid that what you have will be taken. You have to know that you can always replenish it. There's no reason to be afraid; you have to have self-confidence. They believe that we're very capable and adaptable. Yet many fear change. We need to feel that change does not represent increased danger.

Costada on this fear:

There are some people who will try to come and take what you have. What's wrong with that? Is what you have so necessary that you can't let others have it? Why do you feel the need to hoard it? We won't be afraid if we don't think we have something that will be taken from us.

John on this fear:

We can't outfly it. We have to deal with it within ourselves.

Exercise on Judgment

Ask yourself the following questions and write the answers in your journal:

1. Are you worried about other people's opinion of you? If yes, why?

2. How does their opinion affect how you feel about yourself?

3. Has your concern over the opinions of others lessened over the years?

4. Do you ever feel misjudged?

5. Do you judge others? If so, why?

6. Do you judge people on the way they look?

7. Would you like a friend less if they were disfigured?

8. What qualities do you look for in a friend?

9. Which of these qualities do you embody most?

10.   What attributes do you offer your friends?

11.   Do you feel you ever judged someone incorrectly?

12.   After this contemplation, can you imagine releasing your judgment of yourself and others?

Chapter 14
The Benefits of Good Manners

"The humble are they that move about the world with the lure
of the real in their hearts."

—Wallace Stevens

Politeness is a way to show love for another person. Treating them
well and with respect makes them feel happy. Good manners are
a way of interacting with another being and you both come away
feeling better, happier, and more peaceful. You lift each other up.
The showing of respect is especially important because everybody
deserves it. Plus, it makes interactions with others go more smoothly
and enjoyably. Simply put, treat others as you want to be treated.

Costada

Manners, Costada says, are important and people should
employ them. She defines manners as the way we interact with
other people. We don't realize how much power we have when
we talk, so it's important to say the right things. Costada likes
people that have good manners.

Good manners are like a mirror of a relationship. If the
manners are good, so is the relationship. On the other hand, if
you treat someone poorly and exhibit bad manners, then the
relationship can't be good. People will know their manners are

good if when they leave someone, that person is happier and smiling. It is the same with us when we are being treated well.

Good manners can be taught. Remember, we keep learning throughout our lives. Good manners, if we use them, make our relationships better. People like people with good manners. However, Costada says that this is not something most people spend meaningful time trying to improve (she is never critical, so she doesn't say we are wrong if we don't work on having good manners).

She says the topic of manners brought up by the guides is relevant because today's world is spiraling downward; people appear to be meaner to each other, less civil and at times hostile. We should think back to the times when people were polite and treated others with respect. There was a lot more harmony.

Having manners is a way to keep control over negative impulses. As an example, she points out that if you're planning on saying something negative to someone, know that it can really hurt them and it doesn't do you any good. If you have good manners, you'll know not to say something hurtful. She says there is never a reason to say something hurtful. The guides cannot understand our desire to hurt another.

To improve our manners, Costada suggests looking at the times we connected to other people and were moved by a simple act of kindness. Remember how good it felt. She recommends trying to emulate that behavior in our dealings with other people every day. She admits that manners are sort of superficial. It is simply being good to everyone else and sending out positive energy. Most people, she says, understand the word "manners";

it's easier for them to comprehend, rather than hearing the words "creating and spreading high vibrational energy", which is the same thing.

Arcturians

Manners are like habits; they are behaviors we learn that become ingrained in us and make our lives easier. They also act as a buffer for us, so we don't put out negative energy and hurt other people. It is sometimes best not to talk to someone about what is bothering you. They may not be in a place to understand it. It may be better to wait till they are older.

The Arcturians have an interesting view on manners. They say that if you think of people who don't have manners, think about jails. People who are in a tight space often don't respect each other and have the tendency to fight. They say we don't respect each other enough. We have a propensity to put people down, which is wrong. We need to stand up for ourselves, but in a way that is not an attack. They say that unfortunately we often are not good at distinguishing between the two.

It is important that we stand up for what we believe in and for what's right. Yet the Arcturians believe we have to do it as a group. That's when change occurs. That's why we have to have manners – to converse with each other clearly. This is the way to become unified. We are much stronger when we're in a group with like-minded individuals. We are similar to herd animals and we don't like to be alone. The better the manners the more peaceful the co-existence.

The Arcturians say that we are no different than animals, and that we just mistakenly believe we are. They point out that animals have manners. They move over for each other. They call to each other when there's food. They are not mean to each other, at least not frequently. This is called having manners. They are respectful of others. Conversely, we are not always respectful of others. It goes back to the way of thinking that we're better than other people. Animals never think that.

The angels also make the point that if we encounter someone with a lack of manners, we should not let it affect our life. Unfortunately, some unenlightened people thrive by being divisive. We should not let them be effective. People's joy comes from being united. If everyone had manners, there'd be fewer problems.

Manners, they say, are both taught and instinctual. We can always work on learning new manners. The top three manners that people need to focus on are:

1. Be respectful of others. Love them as you love yourself.
2. Help someone who needs help.
3. Spread your joy, but not your pain.

They say if we walk down a path and have good manners, an abundance of flowers will grow up behind us leaving a beautiful trail. But if we go through life with bad manners, we will have nothing but unsightly surroundings. No one good will come into our circle. People on a negative path stay in groups and complain, creating more negative energy. It's not exactly wrong, it's simply a path taken. But we naturally want to take the good path. We can do the same; accelerate positive energy with good intentions and manners.

John

According to John, people with exceptionally good manners are well liked by other people. John says manners are classy, which is something that people should strive for. He said not to worry if we were not taught good manners. We can rely on our instincts on how to relate to others properly. Rely upon those, and it will help improve your interactions with others. Our actions create our feelings. We have to act and feel as good and as positive as we possibly can.

The good thing about manners is that they're one-on-one. It's not the way our country, for example, deals with another country. We don't deal with other countries; we just deal with people individually. John says we shouldn't let politics, for example, upset us because it's not a one-on-one relationship.

Exercise to Improve Manners

1. Remember and apply all you've learned through the years about manners. And continue to be open to learning more through others kind behavior.

2. Emulate the qualities of those you admire.

3. Find joy in being polite and respectful.

4. Find pleasure in making others smile.

5. Hold a door for someone.

6. Say please and thank you.

7. Tell truths.

8. Be helpful.

9. Always be kind.

Most importantly, remember the saying: "Before you speak, let your words pass through three gates.

- Is it true?
- Is it necessary?
- Is it kind?"

Chapter 15
Laugh and Play

"The most wasted day of all is that on which we have not laughed."
—Sebastien Roch Nicolas Chamford

Play is quite important. We should always play and we don't play enough. The definition of play is something that makes you smile. The guides recommend just being silly and seeing its value in making you happy. It produces nothing but pleasure, which one should view as vital to our well-being. It's important to play because it balances out the times we work or worry. We can't work all the time, it's not good for our soul. Playing lets us relax and enjoy ourselves. The guides love to play and they'll give your ideas about things you enjoy doing. You can also play with them. Everything doesn't have to be about learning and improving. Often, it's just about making ourselves happy. That's what play is.

Costada

Happiness is inherent in playing and laughing. Costada says people don't think about playing enough. We never want to lose the enjoyment that laughter and playing brings.

If you can't imagine playing again, just think about being silly. Stop feeling like you have to behave properly. To be able to laugh and play is its own reward. That's what's amazing, the immediate gratification.

Laughter shows you're playing right. It is the result of inner energy coming to the surface and spilling over. We have an unlimited amount of laughter inside of us. Some people allow themselves to be relaxed and happy and laugh. Meanwhile, some people are too serious due to all the chores that we put on ourselves that aren't necessary. Some think that they should be adult and serious, but nobody says we have to. Adults can and should regularly laugh and play.

Humor gives us joy. Costada says that it's a break we allow ourselves as we experience happiness while we are laughing. She explains that some things are funny to some people and not to others, similar to some people being ticklish in certain areas while others are not. Some people find odd things funny. It's all good.

She finds a lot of things funny. She finds us funny because we run around in circles for no reason. We put out a lot of energy for seemingly no cause. They "human watch" and find us humorous, but they don't laugh at us. We're entertaining. Humor, Costada says, will show the life inside of us. We don't have to have heavy thoughts.

The more we laugh, the more joy we have. It can also be a gift you give to someone else, by making them happy. People like that. We're just hard-wired to enjoy fun and funny things.

Humor really is important, it's a variation of playing. It takes the seriousness out of life. We're much too serious, she says. Everyone is funny, she states. Some may appear funnier than others, but that is because they're more willing to open up and share their funny or silly side. Others simply keep it inside.

Costada finds amusement in pointing out areas where we are inaccurate. Our opinion of the Lord is imprecise, for example, as we hope to be reunited with Him when we die. Actually, she says we are never disconnected from the Lord; he is right beside us and in every cell. She finds it funny we don't know this.

Arcturians

The Arcturians do not seem very funny. However, that thought made them quite insulted. They think they are quite funny and witty. Once, spaceships came up and the Arcturians just kept laughing at how we humans complicate the simplest things. We do not travel by spaceship; we travel by lives.

The ability to laugh and play is affected by our upbringing. Were we told to be serious or run around and be happy? Did we run all around and play in the grass? We can retrieve the happiness of our youth by stripping away some of the serious adult layers. The Arcturians recommend that people start by taking off their jacket, loosen their tie or scarf, and kick off their shoes and socks. Then we can run around and play in the grass again.

John

He just doesn't understand why people aren't laughing all the time. John says when we laugh, it's like we fly high.

He thinks that other birds and animals are funny. He likes to watch them chase each other and run around, and he really loves it when they stumble and fall. But the soft earth keeps them from getting hurt. John laughs when he watches animals try to eat eggs. Eggs are the perfect shape. When an animal tries to eat one it just slides forward out of its mouth. He says the bears in particular have a penchant for eggs and also have a great sense of humor. They think everything is funny. It's fun to watch the young bear lie on his back, pull down a branch and then try to catch it as it snaps back down.

Playing
Costada

She believes that when doing activities, they should be done in the most amusing and easiest way possible. This is an important lesson to learn as it applies to all of life. When we have the choice, always choose the fun, easy path. This can be accomplished by letting down our barriers and just feeling what is the most enjoyable.

Avoid the path that feels difficult and anxious. If life is hard, we should just change direction to what's easy and fun. We will make a lot more progress and be more prosperous. If you believe there's a problem in your life, you might find yourself worrying about it. This yields nothing positive. One strategy is to just put it out of your mind and think of something else that will make you happy. Become totally engaged. You'll feel good and then you can work and be very productive as a result of being in a high vibration. Then it won't take long to get everything done and you'll feel really good and proud of all you've accomplished.

Everything we do, we should enjoy. If it's not enjoyable, we should just stop. If it's a chore we need to accomplish, and don't want to, we need to change our perspective. To do this, imagine going through the chore step by step. Determine what you dislike the most. See how to eliminate it or complete it with acceptance. No need to feel sorry for yourself, it is a chore you have chosen to complete.

Meditation Exercise for Fun

Chapter 16
Freedom

"My days have been so wondrous free
The little birds that fly
With careless ease from tree to tree,
Were but as blessed as I."

—Thomas Parnell

Freedom is one of our best gifts in life. We're totally free to do anything we like. We can move our body when and how we choose; we can learn different things and we can go exploring. We can do whatever our heart desires. Unless they are locked up, every creature is free. Everybody should feel the excitement and thrill of so much freedom.

Arcturians

The wise Arcturians say our souls are free. We are free. We have no limitations; we only think we do. People who do not feel free should realize that it is all in their head; it is imaginary. We just have to know that there is nothing we cannot do. Bring in positive thoughts. Get rid of any self-defeatist attitude. We all have the ability; we just have to get out of our own way. Stop limiting yourself by returning to old habits, negative thoughts and poor behavior.

The best way to get out of our own way is to choose where we want to be and what we want to do. Know that we have the power and the freedom to do it and we should not put up roadblocks because there's really nothing to stop us. If you feel there is something you cannot do, meditate on it, and your guides will provide you with the solution.

Emphatically, they believe we really are free to do anything we want. We are not our chores and we are not our obligations. They are our choice. We just see them as chores and jobs and that's wrong. We are free. Everything is within our power. We can do anything we choose at any time and we should only do those things we want. That is freedom.

There are effects or consequences from which we may want to be free. At times, when we are in severe pain, we want to be free of our bodies. Instead, we should focus on being free of the pain. To help eliminate pain, the Arcturians suggest meditating about being outside in nature. Just imagine that you can walk outside by a grove of cherry trees. They are in full bloom, the weather is sunny and beautiful, and the temperature is perfect. It's all for you and it feels so good to be free in the outdoors. Notice how the pain fades away when you feel the sensations of a beautiful sunny day. They say when people are in nature, they are completely free. Just like everything else in nature. Know you're free and feel it.

John

According to John, some people don't think they have freedom, but they do. He suggests that you spend time concentrating on why you think you're not free. He is incredibly sad about the people in jail. Most people are free and can do anything they choose. You should just take a moment and think what it is you want to do most – and then do it.

Costada

Costada interprets freedom as the means to do whatever we want. We have no obligations. This means that there's nothing we have to do, just things we want to do, like taking your kids to school every day. It's not a chore, but something we choose and want to do. Everything in life should be exactly as we want it to be. Even something like scrubbing a pot can be easy if you just let it soak. Find ways to make your daily activities not seem like chores. If you take your time, it won't be a chore and let yourself feel a sense of satisfaction and pride when you finish the project.

Costada interprets freedom as the ability to fly. It's called astral traveling. She said we all could do it any time we want. Astral travel is when you leave your body and go someplace else. She said we do it occasionally at night when we sleep.

Its purpose, she says, is to provide the closest thing we can get to being home. We can just zip around wherever we like and it's very natural for us. To experience it for yourself, she says you have to get into a very deep trance and then picture where you want to go. She recommends at first not to go too far from where you are.

Costada suggests going into a trance and imagining entering another room. You can walk into the room or go through the walls. She said that astral travel is for advanced people, although anyone can try it, and it is best done with a hypnotherapist trained in astral travel. She also suggests that when you do your body scan, at the end rise above your body and look down at yourself. See yourself filled with the color of the light you choose. See if any areas are highlighted that need attention. This is astral traveling above your body.

Arcturians

Arcturians tell us that astral travel is when you meditate and imagine going to a beach, for example. It's just as good as being there. You can feel the sun, the warmth, and the water. You can be there in just a moment's time. That's what they consider astral travel.

Exercise for Feeling Freedom

In your journal answer the following questions.

1. Define what freedom means to you.

2. Are you free?

3. How can you feel more freedom in your daily life?

4. Do you feel you have obligations that weigh on you?

5. Can you eliminate or decrease these obligations?

6. Can you view some as choices rather than obligations?

7. How can you progress to a place of feeling free?

8. Name three things that will help you reach your goal.

9. Explore your past lives to discover if you were enslaved before and if it is still affecting your soul.

Chapter 17
Adventuring: The World is Our Playground

"To see a world in a grain of sand and a heaven in a wildflower, hold infinity in the palm of your hand and eternity in an hour."

—William Blake

We were born to have an adventure. That's why we're here. We can make it as exciting and fun as we want. By opening our eyes to new things that we didn't know existed, we can see new ways of behaving. We'll feel connected to the earth and to the other souls we meet on our journey.

John

John says the world is ours and we are meant to go adventuring. He recommends exploring in trance. His first suggestion is to go to the Amazon rainforest because it is teeming with life and natural beauty. There is an abundance of lush greenery, beautiful lakes, and rivers, and so many fascinating animals. He says it's the healthiest place. He says we can see creation there. We will be able to experience how everything comes from nothing and becomes a beautiful living thing just like we do. The lesson is that we can grow into anything we want.

That includes being able to heal ourselves. Know that every day that we're growing and getting better, just like everything else in the Amazon. We're flourishing. Bring yourself one image of the Amazon with you that shows how everything thrives since it has everything it needs already. Just as you do.

Next, we can imagine that we are floating in the air. We can go anywhere we want to go. When we arrive at any place on the earth, we can just go there and explore. First look at the big picture, and then go down and look at the little, tiny things. See the wonder all around us.

You can also go adventuring in a beautiful green land. Look at the colorful stones on the ground. They're so powerful. They can talk to you. You are here to discover their power. We should realize that there is power in everything. The power, John says, is the power of connectivity. We are all connected. The more you get to know your world, the more comfortable and joyful you'll be and the less fear you'll have. So, go adventuring, but do it slowly so you can appreciate it.

Arcturians

You need to trust and have patience. It's getting easier and easier because everything is just working out perfectly. Adventuring and meditation can change a life around. An affirmation to help you remember your adventure is to love everything and know you are worthy to realize anything you desire.

The Arcturians say that the world is our playground – essentially a happy place. We should be out there playing and know we are never too old to do it. A wonderful adventure they recommend is to imagine sliding down a rainbow, going down each of the different colors one by one.

Adventuring is fun to do while in trance. To begin, climb up a gently sloping hill. Find a place to relax and look out at the distance. Fill in all the details, the colors, movement, sounds, scents, feelings, the land, foliage, water, animals, and birds. Feel all the clean, positive energy coming from this magical place.

We're meant to wander. The Arcturians say that everyone, when not in a trance, should take 20 minutes a day and just wander some place. Also, know we are never lost; we are always exactly where we are meant to be.

Costada

Costada says it's only when we go adventuring that we find new things. It's easy, and you don't need to travel far. She suggests going adventuring in a trance. This is better than adventuring in real life because you can explore anything and everything, while having the benefit of getting answers from your guides to questions about what you have found.

It's so important to make new discoveries which is why it's so vital to explore. The experience will make us all feel wiser and we will gain new knowledge the more we discover. We should make curiosity part of our daily routine.

Seeing and experiencing new adventures makes our minds better. With all the variety we can see, the more we can grow and the better we can reason things out. We should try new things, either alone or with a few other people. Costada tells us that adventures create the best memories and they're fun to relive. She's simply into us trying something new.

Technology
Costada

Costada explains that too many people are playing two-dimensional computer games. She's not a fan of computer games. They don't provide any memories or knowledge. As for the new virtual reality glasses that allow people to see three-dimensional images, she does not like them. It's better to see it with our own eyes in three dimension and touch with our hands. You can't make a connection with technology. She says a computer is dead, it has no energy. It's not like a tree.

Exercise for Urban Adventuring

1. The angels say we should go on adventures wherever we live.

2. If you are in an urban area, walk down other streets or parks you haven't explored before.

3. You can even explore the rooftops.

4. Walk slowly, and remember to look up and all around you.

5. Climb hills and steps to view things from a different perspective.

6. Adventures can be had in places we have been before if we see them through a different lens.

You are blessed if you live in the country and are close to nature. Go adventuring upon the soft earth. Walk slowly and see what you can discover. The angels say there is always a lesson to be discovered and learned.

Chapter 18
Finding Your Life Path

"Change everything, except your loves."

—Voltaire

The whole reason we are here in this life is to find our correct path, thereby being able to grow and learn the lessons we need to know. Everyone is able to find their life path. Listen to your instincts and your desires because they're pulling you toward the right direction. People will know if they're on their life's path because all their dreams are coming true. It really is the ultimate way to live your life joyously.

Costada

Costada affirms that we are born with a predetermined life path. We do, however, have a tendency to stray from it. Most people aren't completely on their right path. When we are on it, life couldn't be better. Everything flows smoothly and enjoyably. When we are in alignment, we just drift around obstacles and negative energy has truly little impact on us. The solutions to problems become obvious.

We can obtain clarity about where we are relative to our path by assessing how we perceive, react and cope with obstacles that we face. When we stray off our life path, things can go awry. We're anxious and our mind races with negative thoughts.

We can get depressed. We have to realize that we haven't done anything wrong, and we've just gotten off our path. Luckily, Costada says there are many methods for getting into alignment and back on our right path.

She says it's amazingly easy to find our correct path. Everything that is positive in our life is pulling us back to our correct path. So, whatever you like, you should run towards. Avoid those activities that bother you. Listen to your gut, your instincts – they are all pulling you back to your correct path. If you're satisfied and happy, you are on the right path.

Costada says sometimes we can go extremely far afield from our correct life path. That is when anxiety and depression creep in. If we feel lost, Costada advises us to look back at the dreams we had when we were younger and see if they still hold appeal. If they do, we should see how distant we are from obtaining that goal. It's much harder to reach your goal if you don't know what it is or if you're not on your right path. Think about what would make you happiest and aim for it.

We don't have to be concerned if what makes us happy is good for us. If we enjoy it, it is good for us. It's that simple. But don't get confused. For example, if you don't want to work, but like the pay, then work is actually something you want to do. Or if you enjoy cupcakes, but believe they are bad for you, eating them is not truly making you happy.

We can tell if we are on the wrong path because we don't feel fulfilled. Costada suggests contemplating about what is not satisfying in your life. Meditate and ask what is missing and how you can find it. Doing so will help direct you toward your path.

She says it's particularly important to stop what you're doing if it feels amiss, because you're just going further afield.

Through meditation you will see your path and determine if you are on it. Try to walk towards it and see what feelings arise. Always ask your guide for assistance in finding what your life path is. Costada says there is nothing wrong if you encounter obstacles along the way, as obstacles are learning experiences. Every time we overcome one, we grow stronger and become wiser. Don't attempt to fight or plow through the obstacle. Instead, try to accept it and work with it. You will come out the other end stronger, more self-confident, and prouder.

We might be dealing with subconscious obstacles that we don't know about. Again, we can find out what they are through meditation. It's important to get to the primary cause or trigger that led to the subconscious block. Costada recommends doing regressions to find out why you have obstructions. The cause might be from your past. Meditate and ask to go back to the life event that caused you to feel "off" in some way (a relevant meditation is recorded in the chapter on Anxiety and Rebirth). Ask your guides to show you the event that steered you toward the path you are on. Ask them what you need to do to redirect to your proper path.

When doing the regression, chances are you will be younger but still in this earthly life. Alternatively, you might do a past life regression. You really have little control of where you are when you go to the past. But your angels are with you the whole way. There is absolutely nothing to be afraid of. It's your own private adventure that is leading you to your answers. You will easily know if it is a childhood or a past life regression.

Lastly, Costada says that knowing we are not on our correct life path is fine, as long as we are aware of it. However, she suggests we not stray too far, as it may take years to return to your correct path. She says this is perfectly okay too.

Arcturians

Arcturians define a life path as the track our soul is on. We come to this planet, this life, and are born with our life path already in place. They say that when we're on it, everything is joyful, so let it pull you towards it. It has tremendous power, one's life path. Sometimes we get in our own way and struggle against it, but this is not the correct thing to do. If what you are doing doesn't feel right and positive, it is safe to assume you are not going in the best direction.

If our life is going smoothly, it shows we're on our right path; if everything is in disarray, we're off it. It has nothing to do with the age you die. For example, dying early doesn't mean you were off your life path. Remember, we are eternal beings, so the age we die at is not relevant. We choose to be born and are meant to die, and that's not a terrible thing. The length of our life isn't important. The Arcturians say it's not sad when friends, family or even little children die. The hard truth, they say, is that we are wrong to be sad. It is not wrong to miss them. It is just important to remember that once we die, we are so happy to be home again among our loved ones.

Interestingly, they say our life path is the same in each life we have. Every time we have a life experience, we're meant to go in the same direction. Every time we come back, we have more experiences. But sometimes we stray too far from our path and we don't have a good life.

The Arcturians say other people's paths do not intersect with ours. They can just parallel ours. This is so no one can actually sway us off our path. We are the only ones with that power. So, if we say it's someone's fault, we're fooling ourselves – we're letting them do it to us. We have to love ourselves enough not to allow other people to hurt us.

One method to find your life path is by listening to your body, or said another way, your instincts. Our body is constantly growing and regenerating. It is perfect and knows exactly how to work. Sometimes, we override our body with force of will and get in its way. When this occurs, our body gets hurt. The Arcturians say we should always listen to our body.

There are times in our lives when we have physical ailments. Just because we become ill does not necessarily mean we have strayed from our path. Some illnesses are on our path so that we can learn from them and come out wiser on the other side. In addition, as we learn to take better care of ourselves, we learn healing methods that can benefit and treat other people.

Sometimes, injury or illness can indicate that we are not on our correct path. The Arcturians say it is easy to tell the difference. When we have drifted from our path, negative events will befall us. It's not uncommon for us to injure ourselves when we are off our path. That is because we did a certain movement and didn't listen to our body's objection, resulting in pain. We may always have residual discomfort because we did not heal properly, but that is just to remind us not to repeat the experience. Therefore, don't let your mind try to take over, your body knows more. If we are off our path, we are not listening to our body properly.

Be joyous and know that the energy surrounding you is positive and pulling you towards your correct path. We have a natural tendency to find it, and it becomes easier with each passing year.

Meditation for Finding Your Life Path

Chapter 19
Seeing Positives versus Complaining

"Can anyone remember when the times were not hard and money not scarce?"

—Emerson

Seeing positives as opposed to complaining just means what side you choose to swing on. You can see the positive things or you can swing down and see the other side. It's all the same reality. To shift perspective, realize that you have the power to make a choice and it's always better to look at the positives. Only you can make the difference. When you realize enlightenment, you'll only see the positives.

Costada

Life happens and negative events occur. How we respond to these events is within our power. It is common to complain about many things. Pain, nervousness, the weather, our jobs, waiting in line – it could be anything. From Costada's viewpoint, we should stop complaining and look at all the wonderful things there are in life to be happy about.

We are always protected by the Lord, our angels, and our aura. Any negative emotions from other people will bounce off our aura if we keep our vibrational energy high. The negative energy from others can have no impact on us. If someone says something to you that is hurtful, you can decide not to let it in. Remember, negative comments usually say more about the speaker than about you. Complainers exude low or negative vibrational energy. We should try not to let comments affect us by avoiding people who complain frequently.

Costada explained that by not complaining, we are much happier, and it makes the people around us happier. Furthermore, a non-complainer will keep attracting good people who are in good moods (high vibrations). Complaining is useless. If you are complaining about your pain, the actual complaining doesn't relieve the pain, and talking about it only gives the pain more negative power. Costada reminds us that it is within our power to change the scene whenever we find ourselves complaining or when someone near us is complaining.

She says there are only two choices, complaining or thinking positively. Attitude is important. The quality of your thoughts reflects the quality of your life. Acknowledge that your thoughts are within your control.

Costada was very clear when she described that we should have within us a center of happiness that no one's negative words can penetrate. You know that happiness is more powerful than negative words. It actually might make you happy to try to help the negative person be more positive. However, be aware that some people enjoy being miserable and we should just let them be.

One can tell the difference between someone who enjoys being miserable versus someone who needs help. If a person is simply wallowing in their sadness, they might not want your help, but you can still offer it. We all need help at times, but sometimes people build up concrete barricades around themselves. We're not able to help them because we can't break through. In this instance, we should just let them alone. Remember not to let their negativity affect you as people will be attracted to you because of your positivity.

She went on to say that we should look for the good in all things. This can be accomplished by exploring the world more. If you spend time in nature, you will notice that there's nothing wrong, no trees are bad, no little animal is bad, and we're not bad. It's all good.

Arcturians

The Arcturians have a slightly different approach on how to make unhappy people achieve happiness. Just being happy and entertaining people is not the way to go about it. If they are not participating, they are merely watching you try to lift their spirits. Instead, try to ask them questions about their life, and listen to their answers. Let them find out what's bothering them and how they can overcome their feelings of unhappiness. Mostly people just need to talk and be heard. Attention is the key.

They say happy is our normal state. We lose it at times when we load ourselves down with too much nonsense. Or maybe we are dwelling too much on a specific event that is dragging us down. We should just leave and put it all behind us. Be aware that the negative event is in the past and that it need not have any impact on the present.

If we are unhappy and have no one handy to talk to, we should remember that our angels will be there to listen to us, because they are always there. After all, our guides can usually be better to talk to than another human because we can ask how to solve a problem and the guides will provide a concrete answer. They simply listen to us without judging and enlighten us as to what is in our best interest.

John

John offers advice on how people can help themselves to be happy: he suggests having a party. When a crowd of people gather together and enjoy themselves, everyone is happier. You will be especially happy if you are in a high vibration state, thereby bringing everybody up! He says if someone's in a bad mood, push them into the pool, "Shock them out of it." When we asked if he had any gentler advice, he said, unenthusiastically, "You can nudge them a little bit." And he's right. People are happy at parties.

According to John, if someone's unhappy, they're probably living a somewhat solitary existence. There could be many reasons for their low vibration state. To raise one's vibration level, we should spend time with other people (preferably with a higher vibration) and with nature. Gradually this should elevate our mood, lessen depression, and push us to follow our desires. If people start exploring their world, they will leave their unhappiness behind. At times daily life gets in the way, so there will be ups and downs, but when people go out exploring, it just opens the mind to new possibilities. John says people should be open to new experiences. For example, if you are at a party and don't know everyone, startup conversations with people you don't know. He's also big into hugging, but that should be reserved for people you do know.

Exercise for Getting to Know Your Unhappiness

Sit comfortably and ask yourself the following questions. Write the answers in your journal.

1. How happy are you on a scale of one to ten?

2. Does recalling events from your past make you upset or happy? Ask yourself why.

3. How do you feel about your future?

4. Does thinking about the past or future change them?

5. If you are unhappy, stop and think about what is causing your unhappiness in the present.

6. List the top three things causing your distress.

7. Close your eyes and rate how distressful they each are on a scale of one to ten.

8. Focus on the most upsetting. Assume it's a five.

9. Allow the distress to escalate and take it up to a six.

10. Then a seven. Now you're feeling really miserable.

11. Now take it back to a six.

12. Then back to a five.

13. Then to a four.

14. Finally take it to a three.

15. Notice the profound power you have over your feelings and feel the pride and comfort it brings.

16. Know you can utilize this power whenever you wish.

Chapter 20
Corralling Negative Thoughts

"Distrust all in whom the impulse to punish is powerful."
—Friedrich Wilhelm Nietzsche

Negative thoughts need to be contained. Imagine them individually racing through your brain in all directions. Instead, you need focus. Just lasso them and herd them back to the corral, so to speak, so they don't run wild. You have the power to gain control of your thoughts, they don't have control over you. You also have the power to eliminate negative thoughts entirely.

Costada

Everybody does it. Costada says that we all talk to ourselves. It is important to do and it is something we do constantly. It's vital to be aware of this because our inner thoughts have a profound effect on our happiness.

Some of us are not particularly good at self-talk. At times, we put ourselves down. If you have criticizing thoughts, try some of the following exercises. First, imagine what your guides would say about you in this situation. Just for your information, guides are never critical of us. If there is something they would like us to stop or change, they tell us with love and advise us on how to achieve the change.

Second, she says that if we find ourselves upset, anxious, depressed or in any other low vibrational state, we should try to think about what caused us to feel bad. Try to figure out when your mood changed for the worse and what you were thinking about when it changed. Next, go back to those thoughts and see if there's any truth to them. Know that you haven't done anything wrong. That does not mean you are correct. It simply is.

She also says we should challenge ourselves to think of what would make us feel better; in other words, we should make a concentrated effort to refocus our minds on something we would like. In her opinion, we are fairly good at this and can usually think of an appropriate answer geared to what we want in order to make us happy. These steps will teach us how to stop negative self-talk. This will lead to less depression and sadness.

Negative self-talk can arise when our inner voice reminds us of a time when we were young and afraid. The voice tells us "we can't" or "we shouldn't" – or that "something bad will happen." The voice is persistent. But Costada says we must tell ourselves that the situation we are thinking about was a long time ago, when we were young. We should concentrate on the present. We can take care of ourselves. The Lord and our guides are with us, and we have faith and trust in ourselves that we can handle negative events that might come our way.

She says we need to focus on letting the positive energy in and keeping the negative energy out. Most animals and plants do not have any negative energy, but some people do. People are attracted to those who are full of positive energy. Negative energy, on the other hand, is a drag on people's feelings, so they're always trying to get rid of it. Unfortunately, one way they do this is by complaining and thereby sharing the negative energy.

According to Costada, the best way to avoid negative energy is to simply ignore it. It might be a good idea to see if there's any lesson to be learned from this negative energy, but it's not likely.

Another approach is to just remove yourself from the source of the negative energy. Politely walk away.

Arcturians

We can all have a negative voice in our head that focuses on self-criticism and can lead to depression. However, the Arcturians say that we should grow past that stage and transform our thoughts to positive ones. Get a different perspective. We can do this by examining our thoughts to see if there is any truth to them. Most negative thoughts, they say, are not based on fact. Rather, they can result from dwelling on your actions in the past that you find upsetting. However, memories are poor and usually don't reflect your actions appropriately and proportionally. Focus on the fact there is no benefit from dwelling on sad, past events. Negative thoughts regarding the future create anxiety, but again, yield no benefit.

The Arcturians say we are not inherently "bad" at all and that we shouldn't let ourselves say we are. They say we make this mistake because we are "young" while we are living on this beautiful, but primitive, three-dimensional planet. Nonetheless, and most importantly, we can still learn vital life lessons. When we are having a negative thought, we should take our left hand and put it over our right hand and know that our guides are beside us and holding our hands. We are not alone and we are much loved. There's nothing to fear.

If you want to help someone who is plagued with negative thoughts, ask them these questions: What is the basis for these thoughts? Why do they focus on the worst-case scenario? They should go back to the time in their life when the negative thoughts began. They'll see that they might have taken a wrong turn off their path and started to have beliefs that are not correct. They need to be made aware that negative thoughts are harmful, but luckily, they have the power to control them.

The Arcturians also recommend controlling negative thinking through movement. Do jumping jacks. Start singing a favorite song and dance to it. There are many ways to stop negative thinking, but physical activity works well. If one changes what they are physically doing, their thoughts change as well.

Unfortunately, at times the self-talk is a repetition of what someone else has said to us. This can be extremely dangerous. The Arcturians say not to let anyone's negative comments into your energy circle. People's negative comments are simply comments said out loud that they choose to relate to you. You don't have to pay attention to them – just let them bounce off of you. Don't let their negativity have any substance. Instead, have some empathy for the person who said it. The fact that they felt the need to put you down is rather sad.

The Arcturians say it's exceedingly difficult when someone close to us criticizes us; if we care about them, we care about their feelings. However, criticism (unless constructive) is never good.

Instead, we should stand up for ourselves in a positive way and ask the person to stop passing judgment on us, which they have no right to do. We can shield ourselves from their disapproval by remembering how much we love ourselves. When something contradicts your self-love, then it's wrong and you should ignore the comment.

That doesn't mean to ignore the person, just try to help them see life in a more positive light. If you're in a bad place, with negative energy, the Arcturians don't advise sharing it with other people. You can always get rid of it by going into a trance, calling in your guides and asking them for direction.

The Arcturians say that we should work on blocking negative energy. Avoid things we dislike. Set up filters. Unfortunately, some people don't have filters, so they hear the words other people say, take them to heart and start to believe them. This makes them feel small and inferior. It also makes the other person feel more powerful, which is a totally misplaced feeling. Sometimes it's necessary to remove people from our circle but do it gently and with love. So, another method of blocking negative energy is just not being there as a target.

John

Much of our gloom and doom self-talk is like all the birds in the trees squawking at once. It's wasted energy, means nothing, so just stop. It's that simple.

If you are stuck having cynical thoughts and it seems like you always expect the worst, be comforted by knowing that we are a part of nature. Nature is always changing. For example, the weather is always changing and so are we. Nothing is permanent.

A bad attitude will end. Lack of confidence will be replaced by self-assurance. Sadness will turn into joy. Everything bad comes to an end. Then we are back on the path to happiness.

John says negative energy is in the breeze; it doesn't stay with us. We just have to let the negative breeze pass us by and breathe in all the positive energy. When negative energy comes from other people, it is so harmful. He says that if you are in a place with a lot of unhappy people, walk away. He reminds us that no negative energy ever comes from the guides or the Lord.

At times, some people have a hard time blocking negative energy. This is because it gets into our head, we believe it and then live with it. This just leads to a cascade of negative events. Remember, we are in control of our thoughts. We need to learn how to avoid going down negative alleys in our mind. Spending time in trance and speaking to your guides will fill you up with positive energy.

Exercise to Decrease Your Negative Energy with Others

1. If you feel critical about someone, think before you speak.

2. Ask yourself if expressing your feelings will accomplish any good?

3. Is the person ready and able to hear you?

4. Are they willing and able to change?

5. Will they be hurt?

6. If you have said it before, and it had no lasting effect, realize that there is no point in repeating it.

Overcoming Grief
Costada

She says grief is wanting something beautiful that we had in the past but is no longer here. Grief is completely natural. If you're used to having someone with you who provides support, for example, and they go away, you feel grief. You can feel like you can't stand on your own – or don't desire to. Many people succumb to it, which is fine.

However, grief doesn't last with the same intensity over time. If never really goes away because the memories of the people never go away. The souls of the people never go away. However, it is not only for people that we grieve; we can also grieve a lifestyle, a job, a pet, our health. There is much that people grieve about.

Costada says it's good to remember what you loved. But there are some breadcrumbs that can lead people out of that forest of overwhelming grief. First, they should leave the forest slowly. No need to rush through grief. Eventually, you will start to see beams of light again in your life. We should follow the beams of light out of the darkness. Sometimes it's someone else's helping hand. Sometimes it's your own happiness finding you again. Keep walking, and as you live day by day you will come to other beams of sunlight. That doesn't mean to forget the person. Rather let their memory fill you up and fill in all the spaces that were left open when they departed. You can redo the meditation on the Faith and Trust chapter, wherein your talk to a loved one who has passed on.

Exercise to Stop Negative Thoughts

When you are having negative thoughts answer the following questions in your journal.

1. When did the thoughts start?

2. What exactly were you thinking about that made you unhappy?

3. What triggered you to think about it?

4. Do these negative thoughts benefit you in any way?

To stop these negative thoughts, do one of the following:

1. Stand up and do something physical. The angels are fond of twirling.

2. Think of what your angel would have to say about you feeling down because of what you were thinking.

3. What would you angel tell you to focus on?

Chapter 21
Overcoming Depression by Encouraging Positive Thoughts

"Time cools, time clarifies; no mood can be maintained quite
unaltered through the course of hours."

—Thomas Mann

Sometimes we let our mind take on too much power. We have to think with our whole body and soul. We have to know that our thoughts are within our control. We can change them and play with them. Imagine that with a broom you can sweep all the negative thoughts out of your head. In their place, you can plant positive thoughts and let them grow naturally. So, when feeling down, repeat to yourself, change your thoughts – transform your life!. Being able to control and change our thoughts is no small feat; it's a life-changing event.

Costada

Costada says that depression and unhappiness is within our control because we are naturally meant to be happy. The energy is lighter. Thus, it allows us to have the liveliness to do more things. Sadness uses up energy and keeps us from being able to experience joy. It also makes jobs we must accomplish more difficult because we are unable to focus completely. That's why when we're happy, everything flows easily.

Sometimes we unknowingly allow negativity to creep into our thoughts. People, Costada says, should systematically take a look at themselves and be mindful about what they're thinking; if the thoughts are negative, don't let them continue. Ask if thinking about the subject bringing us down does us any good. It's better to focus on it, determine why we're even devoting time to it and come to a resolution on how to push it out of our mind. She says we spend too much time worrying and that this energy is just wasted.

She explains that people act in a variety of ways and do different things to achieve greater happiness. For example, she recommends that we jump up and down and twirl around and around, just like when we were kids. This, she says, will take out mind off depressing thoughts, as we can't help but smile as we twirl.

The key is learning how to change our thought patterns through self-assessment. Sit down and focus on what you were thinking about when you became depressed. Costada says it will probably be related to your negative thoughts about the past or present. Reflect on whatever thoughts you have, or have had, and pinpoint the part that is making you depressed. When you find it, explore it, and separate yourself from it. Find out the real truth. Know that you have the strength to face it. Costada says you will then see that the way you were thinking was misguided and that you have the power to change it.

Costada also emphasizes the importance of paying attention to our thoughts and daydreams. Enjoy the happy ones. We all have different moods and personality traits. Some people tend to be self-critical and belittle themselves regularly. Luckily, this tendency naturally fades with age. She says there is no reason to ever put ourselves down. If we make a mistake, just don't do it again. Don't feel bad about it, it's in the past.

Arcturians

The Arcturians have another method by which to overcome depression. They recommend going into a trance and actually feeling the place in your body where your spirit guide resides. When awake, you will be able to gently tap that area and feel all the love of your angel tingling within your body.

They say people can overcome depression, but we have to get out of our own head, so to speak. How? The Arcturians recommend exploring the world. Be curious. Walk around and try to figure out how things work. Look at a leaf, for example, and explore how it receives nutrients and sunlight, how it grows and how it changes. You'll find answers and feel proud about how smart you are. Sad thoughts will disappear. But you must get out of your room, your house. Look around. The slower you go, the better. You can't appreciate everything if you move too quickly.

The Arcturians like us to study natural items. You can find wonder in a drop of rain or a blade of grass. There is not that much to explore in a city because of all the concrete and lack of natural wooded land. But if you look up you will see light and sky between the buildings and if you look down you will see bits of life growing up from between the sidewalk cracks. Nature is all around us. The more you discover, the further away you are from your disappointments. As you investigate your world and see how it works, you'll be proud of your insights and you'll want to share them with other people. And you should. Henry Davis Thoreau spent two years bird watching. The Arcturians think that's brilliant (and so does John!).

The Arcturians also described how sharing thoughts with other people can help overcome unhappiness. They say it's like a pie (for higher beings they come up with some interesting analogies). If you keep it all to yourself, it weighs you down; but if you cut it into different slices and share it with other people, it doesn't. Don't keep it all to yourself. In a matter-of-fact way, rather than complaining, you can tell other people what is causing your unhappiness. In doing so, you can free yourself of it.

Another recommended approach to overcoming depression is to write down the issues that bother you. Imagine all the unhappiness inside of you. It travels down though your arm, through your hand, and even to the pen you hold in your hand. All the depression is then transferred to the paper. You should read it over and over until it bores you. The Arcturians say you won't be unhappy about that topic anymore. Every day, you can pick another reason for your sadness and write it down. Eventually, you'll have nothing left to write about. They call this a purifying technique. It takes out all the bad energy.

Writing is particularly healing when we're feeling our worst. As mentioned, we should keep notes together in a journal so we can go back and read them over. By reviewing our notes when we are feeling down, we'll realize we were unhappy before, but that feeling didn't last. So, we'll understand that the negative feelings we experience now will also go away. Lastly, they recommend talking to other people or having a pet. They say that a lonely existence can strengthen depression.

The Arcturians say a kind word can change a life. Words are that powerful. They are equally powerful to the words we say to ourselves. But sometimes the words we use are not true, so we need to be careful. Ignore any false thoughts and work on making them go away permanently. We will know the thoughts are bogus because all negative thoughts are untrue. We don't make mistakes. We could drop something and it breaks, but this is an accident. We just have to clean it up. It's not like we're sinful. We should have judgment-free thoughts. Even better, we should just have love-filled thoughts.

The Arcturians also say we can get over negative thoughts by just asking our angels about them and they'll tell us the truth. The spirit guide knowledge is always positive. We have complete control of our thoughts. We just don't always believe we do. The guides emphasize that we can strengthen control over our thinking by paying attention to our own thoughts more.

The conversation with your angel will enable you to get to know your depression better and the reasons behind it. You then won't feel as sad anymore; you'll be more intrigued. The depression becomes something distant from your being – almost like an inanimate object that you can see and pull apart. Dig around in it, explore and watch it just evaporate.

John

John explained habits. A habit is something that nature gave us to make life easier so that we can go from one activity to another without thinking too much. All animals use them. Along with positive habits, we've unfortunately evolved to the point where we can develop negative habits, like negative self-talk. John says that animals don't berate themselves. Only humans do.

People sometimes think that habits are too much a part of us, and that we can never stop them, but in actuality we really can break free of them. Think of all the ex-drinkers, ex-smokers and ex-drug addicts. Negative self-talk is more difficult because we're always talking, but we can still change the voice in us to a positive one.

For example, if someone says something that hurts your feelings, you may begin to feel bad about yourself, think more about it, and find yourself in a downward spiral. Thinking about what you believe you did wrong is common, but it's not helpful. We do not need to keep other people's negative comments. Instead, we have to realize that our own thoughts and beliefs are more important than someone else's.

John says happiness is in God. God is happiness. John says the Lord loves us so much and he wants us to be happy. Feel his happiness and his love.

Meditation Exercise to Deal with Depression

Chapter 22
Simplify Your Life

"We're never single minded, unperplexed, like migratory birds."
—Rainer Maria Rilke

Simplifying our lives is one of the easiest things we can do, and what a difference it can make! At times, our lives may appear so complex that we feel overwhelmed by it all. We do many unnecessary chores when there's really no need to do them. Some people let various day-to-day issues take up so much time that there is little energy left over for pleasure. To combat this, we just need to slow down and let go of all extraneous and superficial elements of our lives. Then we can relax, enjoy, and explore to our heart's content. Realize how little is actually needed for a lovely journey through life.

Costada

Costada says we need to simplify our lives, take our time, and see more. If we take time to finish a project properly the first time, we won't waste time having to do it again. If we observe more, we will be likely to see things from a different, happier perspective. We might decide to take the time to watch a leaf floating in a stream, enjoy its natural beauty, simply relax, and enjoy the glorious moment. We should envision ourselves as a leaf, gently floating through life, avoiding rocks and other hazards.

She tells us that our minds are not built for multi-tasking. Instead, we should focus on concentration. She recommends writing down a list of items you want to accomplish in a day. If you accomplish one thing, and totally complete the task, you should feel really good. She says if we do too many things at once, the results are usually disappointing. When we are not truly focused on the task at hand, efficiency is lost. The brain can only focus on one thing at a time. If you are working and thinking other thoughts, distraction sets in. You have probably experienced times that while you are concentrating on what you are doing, you find yourself in "the zone" and accomplish amazing amounts in short order.

Costada wants us to be aware of our surroundings, to be deliberate in our actions and thoughts, and to get things done in an orderly fashion. For example, if you are walking out of a room, take a few seconds to look around and see if you've left anything you need to take with you, rather than having to waste time returning for it. This also eliminates those annoying thoughts associated with knowing you have to go back and fix something later.

Planning ahead is another way that we can simplify our life (this was the only time Costada mentioned not living in the moment). Do specific chores on specific days, on a regular basis. This eliminates stress and gives you a sense of satisfaction when you complete it. In addition, straighten up as you go along. By cleaning as you go, and completing the chore, you don't have to come back to it later. Plus, you can look at what you've done and be happy. However, sometimes life gets in the way and you have to alter your plan. A phone call may appear to interrupt you, but perhaps catching up with an old friend was worth it. You enjoyed it. It made you happy.

Another tip on how to simplify your life is to not complicate things. You could wear the same top you wore the day before. You don't have to make sure everything is perfectly coordinated, unless it brings you pleasure. Instead, do what's easy. You should just be happy, stand up straight and smile. You'll appear so much more attractive than if your clothes are just coordinated. Remember the saying, "smile, happiness looks gorgeous on you".

Arcturians

The more we simplify our lives, the less pressure we place upon ourselves and the less we have to worry about. They say worrying can be a fairly pervasive problem and it obviously gets in the way of happiness and prosperity. The Arcturians say worrying is awfully bad for our health as it upsets our natural rhythm. They point out that nothing can get better by worrying; we just waste energy, which is better spent on doing pleasurable things.

Some tips offered by the Arcturians on how we can stop worrying include first talking to your guide. Realize the guides will help you find a reason not to worry. Every moment will take care of itself, just as it has in the past.

Worrying about the future does no good and does not change it. We have no control over the future, only the present. However, the Arcturians remind us, what we can do is control our thoughts – the troublesome, nagging thoughts that cause us to worry. If we simplify things, we open our mind up to more possibilities of spending time doing activities that make us happy. We can change our attitude toward minor issues and not be so bothered by them. We will become lighter and freer. Then we can grow to love our life more as we live in the moment, unencumbered.

We put in a lot of extraneous effort ignoring our natural rhythm, instead of working with it and letting it support our well-being. Not everyone is the same. Our personal rhythm allows us to do what we are meant to do and provides the energy needed to accomplish it. This is not to say that we can't be spontaneous or that we can just ignore certain deadlines. Rather we should pay attention to our energy levels and let that be our guide to what we accomplish. The simpler we make our lives, the less we need to accomplish to be happy.

John

John has simple comments about simplifying. He can enjoy just soaring through the beautiful sky, hardly putting any effort into it. He reminds us there is no need to worry or be anxious. There are ways to get around our worries and find solutions. In his bird's eye view, we should just soar through life letting each moment unfold as it is meant to be.

He says to remember that we have a solid base of spirit guides supporting us. We should be like him and float through life, unperturbed and easygoing. From his perspective, we can get too caught up in little things that are a waste of time and energy.

For instance, do you really need to untangle the chain or can you just leave it? He says we spend a lot of time on useless things, time that could be used to appreciate the good things in life right in front of us, particularly in nature. We could lay down on the grass and see the open sky loom above us or take in beautiful scenic mountains. It might not be flying, but it isn't time wasted; it's time well spent. He says we have it all wrong. We think if we're doing something, like untangling a chain, we are being productive. However, he says it's frequently the opposite.

Exercise on Simplification

The overall goal is to simplify our lives by lightening the load of emotional and physical pressures. One way to accomplish this is to let go of all the extraneous, unimportant items that can get in the way of enjoying life. Identify the material possessions that are no longer needed.

1. Start by decluttering your home. Identify the material possessions that are no longer needed. Trust yourself to know what you need and what you can let go.

2. First, put together everything that's important to you in the center of the room.

3. Next, take a good look at what is left and you'll likely realize that you don't need it all.

4. Costada says everything is so much more beautiful when there's more space and light around it.

5. Imagine your home as a beautiful, inviting place to live.

6. Before you start giving away or donating items, while in trance, ask your guide for direction about what you should eliminate from your life. Once you have your answer, you can comfortably leave unnecessary items behind. Your steps are instantly so much lighter, your home and mind clearer.

7. Your soul knows what is important. The love, the positive memories, faith, and trust.

Chapter 23
Gentleness and Slowing Down

"Nature does not hurry, yet everything is accomplished."
—Lao-tzu

We should love ourselves. One of the best ways to do this is to be gentle and slow in our movements and our approach to each moment. We will find that everything moves so much easier. It's vital to be kind to ourselves. It's what we deserve.

Arcturians

Arcturians are big on advising us to slow down. They say it's a necessity and that we will accomplish much more by doing so. First, we should look at our life and see which areas we are rushing through. Our guides can tell us where we need to slow down. They say that at times we rush because we enjoy counting our accomplishments, but they say it is better to accomplish things slowly and more pleasantly. Make it flow.

Second, the Arcturians emphasize the importance of slowing down in conversations. We tend to rush to respond when instead we should listen more intently and think about what is being said. We can get our point across, but we should remember it's important to talk to one another, not at one another. The result will be much better conversations. Everyone has something to contribute – even young children.

Slowing down does not mean stopping. Stopping is not productive. When we rest, we recharge. When we get tired, we slow down. When we slow down, we can enjoy the moment. Hurrying or rushing through an activity prevents us from enjoying the moment. A slower-paced existence allows us to enjoy each step of our lives. Instead of having a list in your mind of what has to be done on a daily basis, try to accomplish things as they occur to you. Naturally, this is not possible all the time, but in practice we can benefit by doing this. Know that thoughts come to us at particular times for a reason. Focus on the activity, appreciate it, and take your time. If it's not enjoyable, stop. If it is, complete the task. The Arcturians do not believe in multi-tasking at all.

Lastly, if we slow down, we can show more love to other people. More importantly, we can show ourselves more love. Treating ourselves with love should be a permanent goal.

Costada

Costada spoke about gentleness, saying that, indeed, she herself is gentleness. Our focus should be on being kinder to ourselves. Start being gentle with yourself and in a few months, you will be more stable, happy and in less pain.

When it comes to wanting us to slow down, Costada sides with the Arcturians. If you have ever bumped into a piece of furniture and hurt yourself, she says that can easily stop. In her view, slowing down will not only help balance your life but will improve it. We are more efficient when we slow down.

In discussing gentleness, Costada brought up one of the gentlest animal, a deer, to teach us. The deer said that everything flows when you breathe with calm intention. We can integrate this more into our life with a kiss; a kiss is very powerful. Kiss a friend's hand, see how it makes you feel. The deer is showing us how important it is to be gentle; it's one of the most essential things to life. We get hurt when we're not gentle with ourselves.

She went on to say that our physical body would be happier if we slowed down all parts of our life. She emphasized that there was no need to rush. All bodies are meant to move gently and unassumingly, like the deer. Rushing can hurt us, and by rushing around, we expend energy that could be used for healing. When something needs to be healed, we need energy. For example, if you have a sore knee and you go out for a long walk, it will still be sore afterward, or worse. The healing process will take longer. Instead, think about being more mindful about how you use it.

Thinking is another area where Costada believes we need to slow down. For example, if we get upset, thoughts can race through our mind and we might think that something isn't true. If we thought through issues more slowly, we might not draw distressing or incorrect conclusions. Slowing down allows us to focus and we will find that answers will just come to us. It's similar to being able to hear answers from your spirit guides while in a trance.

Costada says managing our thoughts is particularly important; similar to our hands, this is within our control. We should remember this and make an effort to keep our thoughts happy and positive. When we find ourselves in a downward spiral, we should consciously change direction and go upward. We need to concentrate on what particular thought has upset us and determine if our thoughts have gotten far off-track. If we are dwelling on a negative thought, we should see if it's really that bad – because it's probably not. Therefore, when we start to get upset about something, we should consider whether we really want to go down that path. Most likely, we will realize we probably don't.

John

Your thoughts come from your whole body, not just your mind. They can lift you up. Coast through life, get in the flow, and see how well everything works. Soar and just gently float with the currents.

Exercise on How to be Gentle with Yourself

1. Take an occasional relaxing bath instead of always showering.

2. Focus on good, kind skin care.

3. Treat your body gently.

4. Be aware of treating the bodies of the people and animals you love in a tender way too.

Answer the following questions in your journal.

1. Are you moving slower and with more grace?

2. Are you seeing and experiencing everything around you?

3. Are you walking more slowly, exploring and enjoying the little things?

4. If any worries about your past or future creep in, can you allow yourself to release them with love?

5. Are you composed and easygoing with your thoughts?

6. Are you feeling serene and peaceful?

Chapter 24
Patience

"Speak the affirmative, emphasize your choice by utter
ignoring of all that you reject."

—Emerson

*One day I fell and cut my elbow. I don't heal normally due to
medical issues. The doctor said it should heal in three weeks. In
trance, I asked what my elbow wanted in order to heal. Previously
it had always wanted green healing light. This time it said it was
healing just fine on its own; it was healing at its own pace. After
six months, the doctor suggested surgery but my guides said to have
patience. I did, and it healed completely after five years. Having
patience and faith took away the worry, since I was told it would
resolve itself perfectly.*

Costada

When discussing patience, Costada mentions "Rinny", our
cat. He personifies patience. If he wants something, he'll just sit
and wait until someone notices him. He can sit for an hour or
more. Patience has many excellent qualities. Costada said we
can't think of time as having value. Time is more of a gift. There's
no reason to feel we have to rush. Costada says we have all the
time in the world. We are eternal. Being anxious and impatient

is an unbelievably bad habit that humans can get into whereas patience is a wonderful virtue.

Patience, she says, is kindness toward ourselves and others. Therefore, the question isn't how to be more patient, it's how to be more kind. We need to have endless patience with ourselves, and to be gentler and kinder. Lack of patience is only forgetting to be kind to ourselves and others.

She recommended the following exercise for patience. Take an hour and do nothing and see if you enjoy it. Over time and with mediating, you will come to love your own company, if you do not already.

Arcturians

The Arcturians say they are full of patience as evidenced by the fact they stay around humans and it takes us a long time to accomplish things. They say we go in too many different directions, instead of focusing on the goal and letting it come to us. Once we determine what we want, all the energies will bring it to us. We just have to wait. It might take six months or a year or a number of years, but that's okay. That's why life gets better with time.

The Arcturians recommend the following exercise to practice patience: When you ask somebody a question, stay quiet and give the person a chance to think about the answer. We tend to interrupt each other. Do not underestimate the value of good communication in relationships, they are vital to our well-being.

We have to treat ourselves with gentleness and kindness. And we have to have patience with ourselves. With age we tend to forget things. This need not be upsetting if you just focus on living in the moment. And eventually when we forget most things we are not bothered because we don't remember that we don't remember.

You don't have to think about having more patience, just enjoy the current moment and you shall have patience.

John

John says that he simply is patience because all he does is soar in the sky and look down, and he can do it for hours. We are not as good as he is because there aren't that many activities that we can do for hours. That's why, according to him, he has such a good life. He really is right. He feels free and natural when he's soaring and being patient.

There's never a reason to rush. He says a few minutes here and there don't matter. It will help to keep your mind calm. All will happen in its own time. No need to worry about the future. Just go with the seasons because they are slow. Nature know that's the best way. It's better to measure progress in seasons instead of minutes.

We have to put less pressure on ourselves. We should think about having fewer chores we think we have to accomplish. Our lives will be so much easier. We should give ourselves permission not to do something we feel we should. We should stop worrying so much as it is a total waste of energy. Just have faith that it will work out and it will. That's what patience is all about. Patience equals faith and kindness.

My exceptional hypnotherapist, Ms. Heather Zicko has graciously provided the following meditation on Patience.

Meditation Exercise for Patience by Ms. Heather Zicko

Chapter 25
Energy and Time

"Physical concepts are free creations of the human mind, and are not, however it may seem, uniquely determined by the external world."

—Albert Einstein

Energy and time are interesting and meaningful topics; however, our understanding of them is incorrect. We spend time thinking about time but there's really no need since time is endless. Instead, we should focus on energy and base our actions on how much energy we have, not on what time it is. Energy is important and time is not. We're able to tell time internally. We know when it's time to feed the young, ourselves and when it's time to rest. We don't need to pay attention to clocks.

Energy

Costada

She believes we should be more selfish. We need to adjust our activities to match our energy level versus doing things according to what time it is and what chores we set out for ourselves. Energy is real. Time is a man-made concept. When we feel weak, we have to pay attention to ourselves. If we do too much work, it will make us tired or ill. We should know when

156

to stop all our work and just take care of ourselves. The body naturally heals if we don't use up all our energy.

Energy is so important. It should guide what we should do. Our actions should not have anything to do with time. We should just do what we have the energy to do. We will always have enough energy to do what needs to be done. Just realize that not that much needs to be done. We push ourselves much too hard and that just makes our body tired.

Costada says that healthy ways to rejuvenate ourselves include getting enough sleep and taking naps when we are tired. She suggests we rest periodically. We need to keep our focus in order and determine whether to pursue a project based on the amount of energy we have. In this manner, we'll be healthier and happier.

Arcturians

Arcturians believe that energy is both physical and mental. Our energy levels are signals that tell us how much our body and mind can do. We must pay attention to both of them.

Most people don't know they should rest their minds. Some people, however, rest them too much by watching TV and sitting in front of the computer for hours on end. They say the healthy way to rest the mind is focused breathing. Breathe out all the negative emotions, one by one. Breathe in all the positive ones.

The guides are convinced that if we feel drained, we're probably drained physically and mentally. We should never let ourselves get that tired. The key is not to put pressure on ourselves, that's one of the mistakes we make. We can avoid placing pressure on ourselves by regularly checking in with ourselves and our energy levels.

Know that there is no separation between the body, mind, and soul. We are not separate from our mind and our body. Take a moment, close your eyes, and check in with yourself. Realize that if you don't want to do something you typically do, it means you don't have the energy and you don't have to do it. It's perfectly okay. You shouldn't make yourself work when you don't have the energy; just do it when you have the energy, and if possible, the desire.

The worst-case scenario is for some reason you have to work, you're on a schedule and you are tired. The trick is to concentrate. When you concentrate and get into theta brain waves and completely focused, you can accomplish a whole day's work in a short period of time. You have probably experienced this phenomenon. Focus on the task completely and it will be much easier. Know that the more you meditate the better your ability to concentrate becomes.

Those who believe they must work but don't have the energy to do so should simply stop working. Everybody has to determine whether they should keep working or not depending on the actual urgency or need to work, as well as the amount of energy they have to devote to work. If you believe you must work but don't have the energy, take a five-minute break to do nothing and then try to marshal your forces to see if you have enough energy to continue. Do the jobs you want to do the most, first. They'll be the easiest.

Realize that there's a lot of work that we think we have to do, but it would be so much easier if we were more efficient about it. That's why the Arcturians recommend we sit and think before we start a job. Determine what has to be done and what can be ignored. Then think about how you're going to efficiently do the job, then start to work. It's so much easier once you've laid down the groundwork.

Time

Costada

We are eternal. Costada says to take our time, there's no need to rush as we have all the time in the world. It's a big mistake to rush because then we don't have meaningful experiences, we don't create good memories and we can't learn anything.

The best way to remember to take our time is to pretend we are a wild animal, and just wander around. Animals are not in a rush, and they appear to have nothing to do. It is wonderful to watch them, and Costada points out that they are smarter than we are. We have to remind ourselves to take our time, by thinking that we are not above the animals. Rushing is just human nature, and we should try not do it.

Arcturians

According to the Arcturians, time is a human concept. It really doesn't mean anything. The only thing that matters is everything, and it has nothing to do with time. Time is such a small concept. We have the entire universe. Why should we care about a few minutes? Most importantly, they say that taking your time should be a life goal.

John

John says nothing is a waste of time. It's just a waste of energy. That is because we don't understand time. You will notice that time moves extremely fast when you are in a trance. There is no easy way to explain time because we made it up. We think time moves fast sometimes and slowly others, but John thinks it's just a word we came up with. We should pay attention to our energy levels as opposed to a random clock.

John wants to know why we feel we have to rush. He says getting there sooner isn't going to make a difference. It is not polite to keep people waiting for you so allow yourself enough time and know everything will work out. According to John, man came up with time because of the sundial, but the sun stays longer in the summer, so it shows that time is just an invention and not even a good one. The earth changes and so should our time change. For example, when there's less light in the winter, we have less time to do things so fewer things should be done.

Exercise for Prioritizing Chores

1. It's good to get in the habit of writing to-do lists regarding chores.

2. In your journal, write down what you want to accomplish that day.

3. Circle the three most important items.

4. Pick which of the three is the most necessary job that needs to be done.

5. Allow it to ruminate in your subconscious. When you feel the impulse to begin, start right away.

6. Once you finish the chore, give yourself a moment or a small, healthy reward to mark your progress.

7. No need to think it is necessary to do more unless your body has the energy and desire.

8. Focus on the basics, keeping you and your loved ones warm, dry and fed.

9. Remind yourself that when you are aligned for a task, it will take a fraction of the time and even be enjoyable.

Chapter 26
Reality

"Physics tries to discover the pattern of events which controls the phenomena we observe. But we can never know what this pattern means or how it originates; and even if some superior intelligence were to tell us, we should find the explanation unintelligible."

—Sir James Hopwood Jeans

Life is so much fun and there is plenty more of it we have yet to discover. It's really exciting to explore reality because our current understanding of it is quite limited. Reality is so beautiful and complicated and fun! In a trance, we can explore the endless expanse of the cosmos.

Costada

According to Costada, there is only one reality. We, however, live in a primitive three-dimensional world. Therefore, we are only able to see a ridiculously small slice of reality. What we experience is true, but she says there is so much more that we don't know. We shouldn't worry, she says, because after we die, we will once again just be souls with all the knowledge we desire.

Costada says it is important to realize that there are different dimensions. They are all around us and we cannot see them. She tells us that there is so much more existing in the space around us in these dimensions. Our souls have seen it all and will see it again. Unfortunately, we cannot see it with our regular eyes because we only have three-dimensional vision.

A good way to see things from a different perspective is to go into a trance and imagine yourself sitting across from yourself. This other self will be able to see things from a new perspective. She says we are missing too many details, and that everybody should see and focus more. There are layers and depth to things that we overlook.

She tells us that if something doesn't interest us, then we've missed something. So, take a look at it a second time. Keep looking until you see what is really there. There's always something waiting to be found; we just have to look at it with different eyes. We must learn to sense the different energy surrounding all living beings. She says we see reality as very flat. However, in trance, there are many more layers, and everything is much more vivid.

Arcturians

The Arcturians say, "There are so many layers of reality. So many dimensions. You are just not able to comprehend it. Little ones don't worry about it; it will just give you a headache."

Arcturians say that it is okay not to know everything. Just understand that there is so much more to know. Knowledge makes our life better and richer. We can certainly ask questions but we shouldn't feel we have to know everything. We can trust that we will know what we need to know when we need to, as long as we listen. We will know if we have received the true answer and made the correct decision if it just feels right, and all your senses agree.

The Arcturians are extremely interested in déjà vu. They say it is just a curtain that opens up to our past and/or future. We get an image that is just like before. We can look with different eyes and see different things. Déjà vu is one of the few experiences we can have that shows there is more to reality than we know. The Arcturians feel a bit sorry for us because we cannot see everything clearly here in our earthly bodies. They say there's so much wondrous beauty around us that we simply don't know about in this life.

John

Curiously, John does not agree with the Arcturians. He says that true reality is different from the small amount we see. He compares it to scents or colors, noting that there is practically an unlimited number of scents. They are alike in that they all have an aroma. Yet they are as different as they are numerous. It's exceedingly difficult for us to imagine what something might smell like if we haven't experienced a similar scent before. The same is true for colors. The number of colors is practically limitless. There are more colors than we can distinguish. John says it's like that with reality. We can't comprehend the depth and extent of all of reality because we have no reference on this three-dimensional planet.

He says there are many realities and we only see one; the interesting thing is that this contradicts what Costada said. John reminds us that there are different worlds. They are all interconnected, and we can go from one to another. We shouldn't worry so much about different realities as we go from various realities and dimensions in lives between lives, as well as in different lives. He says we can perceive things much more accurately if we're quiet, close our eyes and go into a trance. Our reality then becomes more precise. He says there are times when we examine reality and then mess it up by imposing our own thoughts. At that point, we don't see reality as it really is.

Dark Matter/Black Holes

Arcturians

The Arcturians have discussed the meaning of dark matter and black holes (at first, we did not know what that had to do with happiness and prosperity). They like the fact we have an interest in them. They love our curiosity and love providing us with answers.

Black holes and dark matter, they say, exist in different dimensions. On earth, we are only able to see about 5% of what exists in the cosmos. The Arcturians recommend that we not think about the different dimensions because we are bound to get a headache. Living in this beautiful, three-dimensional world, we simply cannot comprehend the other dimensions. As souls, we have access to all knowledge. But in this particular time, in this light, in this body, we can't absorb or understand all of it. However, that is perfectly okay. There's so much beauty on this planet, we can't take everything in all at once. We have a beautiful world, but we just can't comprehend everything. There is nothing wrong with that. We are limited, and that is just fine.

There is much to be seen inside dark matter and black holes; they're very dense. Their purpose is simple; they are whole other worlds teeming with life on them. There is so much happening. Moreover, we're meant to be there. They're wonderful places. Everybody, every soul, is so close together. Dark matter is fun! The Arcturians remind us that we have lived there many times and have been there during lives between lives.

Intriguingly, while in a trance, they showed a black hole. There was so much light inside. It's bright. It's beautiful. It's like the Northern Lights against a white light background.

Dreams and the Subconscious

Costada

Costada explained the difference between the messages we receive during dreams versus meditation. Dreams and a trance state differ markedly. In a trance, we are connected to everything and are a part of it. Our focus needs to be on one particular thought at a time. However, when we dream our minds are free to float anywhere. It's effortless. It's like being on a journey and letting our mind work through any problems along the way. However, we can't always get answers from our dreams the same way we can get them through meditation because our dreams aren't controlled. Dreams are our minds at play. Meditation is our minds at work.

Costada also said there is no subconscious mind. We have many thoughts. What we call the subconscious is just a series of buried thoughts and we don't pay attention to them.

Arcturians

The Arcturians say we should try to let the subconscious thoughts out. We spend too much time stomping them down because we are afraid. Instead, we should explore all of them. We can accomplish this by picking a topic, sitting down, and staring into the flame of a burning candle. Give yourself about half an hour to an hour. Just keep going over it and you will find a path that will lead you to an answer.

John

John says "subconscious" is a man-made word. It's the part of us we don't listen to.

That's okay. He says many messages are coming at us all the time. However, just the important ones will have a way of coming out on their own. We don't need to tell the difference between what we should be focusing on and random daydreams.

We can tell if we have exhausted an issue if we keep thinking about it in frustration because we can't solve it. At this point, we should either walk away from the problem for a while or try to look at it from a different perspective. Being stuck in a loop is bad energy.

Meditation Exercise on Your Reality

Chapter 27
Unknown Powers

"It is only with the heart that one can see rightly;
What is essential is invisible to the eye."

—Antoine de Saint-Exupery

We have much more power than we know. Some of it is hidden power and some of it is simply unused. We don't let these powers out because society often deems them odd, but that doesn't mean they're not there. These powers include the ability of foresight, psychic abilities, and the ability to sense energy, including other people's energy and feelings. Our instincts are an underused power. People should explore their hidden powers and use them to improve their life.

Costada

Costada says we only use a little bit of the power we have. This is similar to how we only use a small part of our mind. She said that we have two powers but we do not use them: psychic power and the power of foresight. These are in addition to the power to heal ourselves, but that is not an unknown power.

We have the power of foresight, as evidenced in part by our power for knowing what will happen in the future, although we don't fully realize it. We can tap into this power by listening to our instincts and surprisingly, we'll know how something will turn out. She suggests that people look at their past and see they were not surprised that often. In the same manner, they can imagine their future and see that it will be as they expect. If someone has a particularly optimistic or pessimistic perspective, it doesn't change their future, it just changes how they feel about it.

Regarding psychic power, Costada explains that if we let down our defenses, we can feel what other people are feeling about themselves and help them. We can actually feel their energy and thoughts. The truth will be in the feelings, not in the words. Another example of our psychic ability is the fact that we usually know what people are going to say before they say it. Similarly, we can know at times who's calling us when the phone rings.

Everyone is psychic, but some people are more in touch with their psychic ability. She says the best way to develop the power is not to fight it or be afraid of it. We can even learn to rely on it. It all depends on the individual.

Costada also tells us that we have a lot of power in our hands. We just don't realize how important it is. Our hands contain our inner light. We can join our light and our essence with another through our hands. The power of our inner light can heal someone else and make them feel whole, attached, and complete. When we touch others, we should feel wonderful.

Arcturians

The Arcturians argue that we have a lot of power in our voice. They say the fewer words, the better. This is because messages are simple. When we lecture, we lose people. The Arcturians suggest that when you talk with someone, listen psychically to what someone is feeling and think about what you can say that will resonate with them. Ideas and messages will come to you. Let the other person see some truth so they will listen to what you have to say.

Loneliness, they say, can be eliminated if we use our hands and our voice to connect with people. The Arcturians insist that there is so much more that we don't realize. We have all the answers already. We are not, however, asking the right questions. In addition, we are not spending enough time listening for the answers. We just have to learn them. There's no reason to be confused. Just spend quiet time and ask your guides. Knowledge will flow to you.

The Arcturians remind us that we all have power, but we only utilize a small amount of it. We can tell what we're most adept at by whatever interests us. We should focus on an interest that appeals to us and try to develop it. Those that know about the power of hands are attracted to activities like reiki, massage, and physical therapy. When you meditate you can tell your guide you don't know what power you have and ask them to tell you what it is. They will gladly enlighten you.

John

According to John, the power that we have is that we're meant to survive. All the creatures on the planet strive to live. He also says we have the power to envision the life we want and to manifest it. He suggests dreaming about everything you'd like, including all the details. Then know it will come to you.

Light and our Hidden Talents

Costada

We are beings of light. This light fills us and extends beyond our skin. It is part of our soul and forms our aura when we are in a body. This is the light we have during lives between lives when we are just souls zipping around the cosmos. This light is part of the heavens. She said this light is in us, all around us. It's real and it's endless. This is the light of wisdom – the light of the souls.

She explains how our planet is completely surrounded by this light. The light connects all the souls, demonstrating how we are all connected. The light is connected to all the other worlds, too.

Arcturians

We all have lights swirling within us, representing our many talents. We can discover which talents to pursue by following our passion Whichever talent lights up the most, calls to us and feels like home, is where our best talent lies. It is natural to go there. The light will also reveal your "hidden talents'. But they are not really hidden; you just have to let them come forward. Our bodies encompass a multitude of talents. We are wise, connected, successful and able to learn, help and teach others – all we have to do is allow our talents to come out.

The Arcturians say the light is within everybody, but because we have free will, some people are able to stomp it down so that they are just dark on the inside except for a small ball of light. Although these people live in a dark, sad world, they don't have to live that way. The light is never completely extinguished. The key is to find it and let it glow naturally.

Arcturians offer a way that this can be accomplished easily. The light within us is a force that wants to spread out to all of our being. Therefore, it takes constant effort on our part to keep the darkness. However, all we have to do is stop the sad thoughts and they'll naturally disappear as the light spreads out. We must press ourselves to stop thinking dark thoughts and turn our focus to the following: our breathing, the light, and the emotions of the light within. The more we do this, the less we are able to focus on the darkness.

John

John says the light is just everywhere. We are in the light. It's incredibly sad when we try to shut it out. Some people do that because they don't know they have the light within them. They've turned inward, but with negativity. The solution is to turn inward with love, find the light and feel it spread through your body. It takes away the darkness. We have complete control over it. Each time we turn inward, the light spreads out more and more. He says to do that until all the darkness is gone and we will just be glowing the way we are meant to be.

The best way of nurturing talent, according to John, is to let it out. People have a tendency to push down ideas and dreams. That's a mistake because they show us our natural talent. We should pursue that which calls to us. We shouldn't do things that we view as a burden all the time. Our talent lies is what comes easiest. People think that if it comes easy, it's not that hard, but that's incorrect. For example, some people find it amazingly easy to cook and may think everyone can cook, but they're incorrect. We should do what's easiest and what we love the most.

It's important to find our main talent because then we will find our correct path. If we don't let our talent out, we are not on the right path. Usually this is due to fear. He says there is nothing to be afraid of. John says too many people are doing the wrong thing and it shows in their level of happiness. It doesn't show in their level of money. It's important to know prosperity and success are measured in happiness, not dollars.

Exercise to Show Energy Field

This is such a fun exercise, but you need another person and a cookie.

When you have a person and a cookie (or some similar sweet), take the cookie and put it on the counter. Then have the other person stand in front of you and put their arm out. While they resist you, see if you can push their arm down with just one finger on their forearm. If you can't, try using two fingers. Then three, then four. You should be able to push their arm down with your whole hand.

Next, have them pick up the cookie in their other hand. Then again, starting with one finger, see if you can push their arm down. You will be amazed that it takes a different number of fingers. This is because the cookie interfered with your friend's energy field.

Chapter 28
Faith and Trust

"Great men are they who see that spiritual is stronger than any material force, that thoughts rule the world."
—Emerson

We need to know that no matter what happens to us, we'll be able to handle it with grace, calm and intelligence. We need to have faith and trust that all will be well and to know that we are strong enough to manage whatever comes our way. When we have faith and trust, we have nothing to fear. Overcoming fear is an ultimate goal.

Costada

One day Costada suggested faith and trust together as a topic to discuss in our quest to find happiness and prosperity. She says trust is most beneficial for us and that it is an especially important power. We have this power and we should work on using it daily. Trust is the power to know that we can take care of any problems that might arise. We just have to realize that we can. Trusting in yourself is a key factor that helps lead to happiness and prosperity.

There is no reason to worry if we have the faith and knowledge that we can handle any situation. Costada says worrying is one of the worst things we can do to our body. It takes energy to worry but the energy is not being put to any positive use. One topic we worry about is envisioning our lives in the past when we were at a low and anguished point. Imagining that it will come to pass again causes the uneasiness to set in. It is not going to happen again, she says. By focusing on faith in ourselves that our lives will not revert to another troubled time, we will end up happier.

She stresses that just because something happened in the past doesn't mean it will recur. We tend to think that way sometimes which is incorrect. Faith in ourselves should lead us toward believing that, as Costada says, we're completely free to do what we want. Believing is putting our faith to good use. This helps us carry out the jobs we set out to do. Importantly, faith and trust enable us to pursue happiness. It's the flip side of fear. When you have faith and trust together, you can face any fear.

Costada advises that it is important to first start to think about what you want to achieve. Similar to look before you leap don't just start walking. She says we will know when we're on the correct path because we will be much happier, calmer, and less fearful.

Fear is important. We can't be completely rid of fear as it is a natural part of our being. Fear is a feeling of anxiety that actually helps us, as it makes us aware of dangers in the world to which we need to pay attention. Instincts are the best indicators of real peril. Fear is different. It can correctly relate to the current situation or it can be built up out of proportion relative to the actual danger.

Costada offers the following advice about why we do not need to worry and why we can have faith that the future will be as we desire. Look at how often in the past you were either nervous or afraid of what might happen to you. For the most part, it all turned out alright. Know that your future will resemble your past, unnecessary anxiety over nothing. Instead, have faith. Be careful not to stay on a path where you are frequently worried about negative events that might happen since nothing positive for you will be on this path. We need to achieve a balance because for the vast majority of the time, we are not in danger. If we let our nerves get the best of us, we won't be able to enjoy how smoothly life generally flows.

Instincts should never be underestimated. They are always in our best interest. They are inherent and allow us to react appropriately to either danger or safety. This is where trust comes in. We allow ourselves to trust our instincts – our innate tendency to find our correct path.

Arcturians

My good friends and guides, the Arcturians, say that the easiest way to learn to have trust is to look behind you. See the path you have taken. See how far you have come. Remember and revel in all your past achievements. Recall the various uphill battles in which you prevailed and the seemingly insurmountable problems you encountered and overcame. Be proud of all the times you've struggled and then succeeded, going from doubt to self-assurance. The Arcturians say it is very empowering to know that you can always take yourself out of a bad situation and back into the light.

The Arcturians repeatedly stress that the guides are consistently by our side, watching over us. We know they are there instinctively. The more we talk to them and let them in, the stronger our faith and trust in their power to guide us in making our lives better will become.

John

I trust in John and John says he is trust. He has body weight but knows that he can float in the air. He can do this because he totally trusts in himself. He knows that every time he beats his wings, he can soar higher. He never worries because he has faith.

John is concerned about the damage to the body and soul that happens as a result of worrying. He says that humans are incredibly lucky to be at the top of the food chain. We have fewer things to worry about than other animals, and yet we worry the most. John says we can be anxious about the future because we can dwell on it, while most animals just live in the moment. And that's what we should do.

Other people should be the focus of our faith and trust. We often worry about other people disappointing us and instead, we should think about the good things they provide for us. No need to focus on the negatives. Just have faith that things will be good. And it shall be. It's within our control.

Meditation Exercise for Talking to Someone Who has Passed Over

Chapter 29
The Natural Power of Healing

"Force is not a remedy."
—John Bright

Healing is a natural process by which our body is restored to a healthy state. Cells regenerate by themselves. They are tiny machines with tremendous power. Pain is relieved. Healing may take a long time, which can be frustrating, or it can be quick, which is sometimes amazing. Healing can also be brought about through meditation. This allows us to pinpoint the source of our pain or injury and helps us find the method and energy through which it can be healed. If you have been doing the meditations, the body scans have no doubt already helped you heal.

Costada

While I was in trance, Costada started talking to me about our ability to heal. As I have had numerous illnesses, healing is certainly something that interests me. She showed me a picture of a small spring steel coil. The coil represented our ability to always spring back. We can squeeze the coil so it becomes small, but it will resiliently spring back to its original size once we let it go. Much of the time, the same is true for us when we become ill. It happens naturally and shows the elasticity of health. Illness is not negative energy, she points out. It is simply a part of us at that moment.

She says that first we have to realize that there is no separation between our body, our mind, and our soul. We are one in this lifetime. It is imperative that we get in touch with ourselves, including our body. A way to get better is to first find out what is wrong. She really likes the idea of doing body scans and then rising above our body and looking down. The areas that need attention will light up. Rather than taking a pill and masking the symptom, it's much more effective to ask the area what it wants. Then listen for the answer. There will always be an answer for you.

When we find an area that is lit up, she likes us to go into a trance and imagine sitting across a table from the body part that wants attention. We can then easily have a conversation with the body part. Ask the lighted area what it wants or what it needs to be happy. Listen for the answer and then do the best you can to comply. Costada says many people don't follow through on the suggestions from their body. The body knows more than the mind about what is bothering it.

Pain is an example of our body giving us a sign. It's how we communicate that an area needs attention. She says not to complain much or verbalize your discomfort because that will give the pain more power.

When an area is in pain, if you ask it, it will tell you what it wants. It'll be helpful and show you ways to decrease the pain. However, you need to get to the root of the problem and find out why it's happening in order to heal it. Costada says that an emotional issue can frequently be the cause of physical pain. People hide their emotions too much and it can come out in physical pain. Hence this is the reason you find the origin of, or the reason for the pain, and then deal with the emotional pain. Regardless, it is a good idea to see a doctor if the pain persists or is severe.

When you ask questions about a problem within your body, don't be surprised if the answer is that you should see your doctor. Costada says that we need to tell the doctor the truth. It will make their job easier. Some of us have a bad habit of focusing on our pain but then not doing anything to make it better. It gets us upset, depressed and that makes the pain worse.

Compared to most animals, we as humans take the least good care of ourselves. She pointed out that this is partially due to all the chemicals we ingest through medications, pesticides, and food additives. Costada says that we can make a problem better by picturing ourselves at optimal health and then going through our body attending to any area that is preventing us from staying in good health.

Costada stresses that there's always a solution to our health problems and we're always healing. People can benefit by changing their approach to illness. Instead of having a doom and gloom attitude, look at it as something that can be tackled and overcome – a challenge. Any illness is a challenge, big or small, and we must face the pain. This is the body's method of communicating with us. The sensation of pain tells you that something is wrong. But be sure to listen to it in a positive manner and be thankful for the communication and information it provides. Our body, our instincts and our spirit guides will all send messages that will be spot-on and geared to improving our well-being.

Arcturians

From the Arcturians' point of view, we have a tendency to ignore our bodies. Just as it is rude to ignore someone when they ask you for something, they say it is rude to ignore something that wants – and needs – our attention. We should pay attention and not ignore our body when it hurts. The Arcturians maintain we need to be aware of any pain within us and know it's for our own good. Once we accept that the pain is there, we can start to help heal ourselves through a variety of ways. They advise that sometimes we need to just quiet our mind and listen during a body scan.

The main message from the Arcturians is that we can help heal ourselves. Our bodies have a natural tendency to restore good health. It's not necessary to devote too much attention to the healing process, just assume it's there like the air.

Arcturians emphasize that getting sick is not a negative. It may be unpleasant and a situation we have to endure but we are not to blame. The focus should be on loving and taking care of ourselves and concentrating on getting better. We can rely on ourselves, instead of others, because no one knows our body like we do. The more we care about ourselves and the better we treat ourselves the less sick we are. Sickness should not be thought of as something bad, it's actually just a phase we are currently living through. Like the seasons, illness can come and go.

One of the best things about the Arcturians, and all spirit guides, is that when you have pain, you can ask your guide to place their hand where it hurts. Arcturian guides have such large, warm hands. This will make you relax. The warmth seeps into our skin and takes the pain away. The warmth of their hand is powerful as it also enhances blood flow. Blood is the ultimate healer. The guides also send healing energy to the area just by their touch. All the angels want to do is make us better.

Arcturians say that as we learn to take better care of ourselves, we can teach other people about taking care of themselves. We can also learn from them and pass this knowledge on to others. They say we are smarter than we realize.

Worrying while being ill or needing to heal from an injury does no good and is a foolish waste of energy. The Arcturians say that we should remove worry from our lives if we can. We should either enjoy the moment or work on making ourselves better.

Overall, the Arcturians are telling us to get to know our bodies better. This should help us focus inward, thereby becoming more aware of our bodies' physical and emotional needs. This should be a time of helping ourselves. It's not selfish, they say. It's intelligent.

John

John says healing is natural. If the human body couldn't heal, we just wouldn't be here. Furthermore, the ability to heal does not end; we can always heal ourselves more. It's not a battle. We don't have to fight to get better. Our health will naturally improve as long as we continue to help ourselves and give ourselves the time and rest we need to heal. We have to have faith in this ongoing process.

He says some people do not love themselves enough. If they did love themselves completely, they would take care of their bodies' complaints. He says we live in pain, which is wrong. We should pay attention to the discomfort, listen to it, and help it by doing what it requires. Some people believe they need to be strong and silent, and that's a mistaken belief. Suffering needlessly is not good.

The action to take is to commit to better listening to your body's signals and to take the appropriate action. If you have chronic pain, once you accept its place in your life, you can stop letting it affect your life. It will still be there, but acceptance of it will leave you calmer and quieter.

Health just is, according to John. People should remember that when we came into this body, it was lent to us by the Lord as a gift. We should treat it with the love with which it was given to us. We have it for our entire earthly life. It's our home. We should stop finding fault with it and revel in its uniqueness. Everyone's body is beautiful.

This is John's take on how people can best listen to their bodies. He, in fact, says he listens to his own body very well. He takes his beak and cleans each feather. We don't do that, probably because we don't have beaks and feathers. But for humans, he suggests that if our neck hurts, for example, we take our hand and massage our neck lovingly. Touch is particularly important. He says there is healing power in our hands and fingers and we should use that power regularly. In doing so we'll connect to ourselves through being aware of various sensations throughout our bodies.

John insists there are times when we should make a decision to go to the doctor. If you have an emergency, just go to the doctor or emergency room. You cannot cure yourself if you are bleeding, have an infection, a heart attack or an innumerable number of other reasons. The guides love modern medicine. They think it's barbaric, but very good anyway. The future of healing is much gentler. You can expect smaller surgical incisions due to new technology. The immune system is especially important. One can tell if it's weak, if you feel weak. John says if our immune system is weak, we have to focus on our digestive system.

An illuminating message from John is that people shouldn't think about their bodies, they should think about themselves. There's no separation.

How to Love Your Body
Arcturians

The Arcturians say that self-love is really going to change everyone's life. It is particularly important to tell people to love themselves. You'll feel abundant love from your guides while you are in a trance. You will feel a tingling sensation when you make a major breakthrough, find a wonderful hidden fact or idea, or feel the love of the Lord. While you are in a body, self-hypnosis is the closest you can get to yourself and to the Lord, according to the Arcturians.

Take care of your body. Start with the basics. Air. Breathing is the key to entering a hypnotic state. The more you meditate and focus on your breathing, it will become easier and more efficient as your lung capacity increases. Air is also important for our skin. Get some air and light on your body for vitamin D production.

Next is water. You need to drink. You should listen to your body. You do not have to drink eight bottles of water a day. Instead, drink when you have the desire. The objective is not to get thirsty in the first place.

For people with swallowing difficulties, it can be hard to drink without choking from time to time. This can lead to dehydration. An exceptional product is Double Helix Water. It's a small bottle of ultra-pure water that you add to a gallon of distilled water. Double Helix Water has had an electric current run through it, comparable to a lightning strike. This forms stable water clusters that are the foundation for self-healing on a cellular level. Its healing properties are amazing. It is also very appealing and can do wonders for dehydration.

Water is also needed on the outside of our bodies. The Arcturians like us to take long, warm, relaxing baths. This is an example of responding to our bodies' needs and wants.

Food. Eating disorders like obesity and anorexia represent a major problem in America. We can get into bad habits such as eating too much or too little. The good news is that habits can be broken. You also have a secret weapon. Your body is more intelligent than your mind when it comes to food. If you listen to your body, it will tell you when you are hungry. You should eat what you crave. If the cravings are for protein and nutrients, your body is telling you what it wants and needs. If you crave sweets or fat, that's your mind and you can ignore it. Pay attention to the salt cravings as you may be low on sodium. Or you may just have an overdeveloped taste for salt. If you have too much salt in your diet, cut back. Your taste will adjust, and you will no longer crave salty food.

Shelter is our final basic need. This can be a difficult problem for those without the financial ability to pay for a home. Luckily, the majority of the population has some form of shelter. The guides say we work too much, and we do not take time to relax, play and strengthen relationships. However, we need to work to pay for the food and shelter. Check to make sure you are not working all the time. You need to simplify your life if you are. Work for the pleasure of it if you like your job. Or at least work for the pleasure and necessity of the pay you receive. Don't work just to have more possessions. Life is meant to be enjoyed.

Surgery

The opposite side of being gentle with ourselves is to have surgery. However, it is necessary at times. The guides say that before having any surgical procedure, meditate and do the following exercise. Ask your guides to stay with you in the operating room and ask the Lord and your guides to direct the surgeon's hands during the procedure.

John

John answered first when we spoke about surgery. This was odd as he is usually the last to talk. He was first because he sensed his message was the most important. He said that he or someone else's spirit guide would be needed when we go into surgery. He said this guide would stay at the end of the bed and protect us during the surgery. He said, as a spirit guide, his job is to protect us. He said the angels take this role very seriously.

He said that after a successful surgery, the doctor might talk about how easily and precisely the surgery went. He said the doctor will feel enormously proud of themselves for doing such a good job. The doctor will not know that you asked the Lord and your angels to guide their hands.

Finally, he spoke about being emotionally prepared for surgery. One way to do this is to come to terms with the fact that you will have pain afterwards. So be sure to have enough pain medication waiting. Also, be prepared. Have food and other necessities at home for when you are recovering. These steps will help ease your mind.

Costada

Costada also says it is important to prepare for surgery emotionally. She says our spirit guides are constantly with us, holding our hand. When we're in the hospital, she says to meditate, and the guides will be there to help make the pain go away. Your feelings of fear and anxiety will be lessened because your guide will always be with you. She says not to do much the week before the surgery and to try not to worry, as focusing on it will not yield any positive results.

If you have had biopsy surgery and are waiting for the results, it can be a stressful time. She says hypnosis is a good way to distract ourselves until we get the results. She says to focus on receiving positive news. Regardless of the outcome of the surgery, your guides and your body know how to heal.

Arcturians

The Arcturians also gave an emotional pep talk. They said to look at the worst-case scenario and know that it's really not that bad. They said to accept whatever is wrong with your health. Acceptance of the inevitable is vital. You have to love yourself, illness and all.

They also gave awfully specific post-surgery advice. The Arcturians say that when your body hurts during the first days of recovery, you can put ice on the hurtful area. Regardless, know that after a week the pain will be much less. Next, they suggest meditating and going to your own beautiful, private beach. Imagine yourself lying down on the warm sand, deeply relaxed as you sink into the warmth of the sand. Feel the sand between your toes. Hear the gentle sound of the water and feel the breeze. Bask in this magical healing sunlight. It relaxes your entire body. Remember, your guides will be with you and they can help you through the pain of following days.

Balance Issues
Arcturians

We may not all be gymnasts who excel at the balance beam, but according to the Arcturians, there is a simple solution to ordinary, everyday balance issues we encounter. We can avoid clumsily walking into objects or walls, suddenly misstepping, or complaining about not being able to walk even a city block simply by slowing down. If you start to walk faster and bend forward, it can feel easy to do at first. This is because the forward momentum makes walking seem simpler and more effortless.

However, this is not a good practice. You have less control over your balance if you use momentum to walk quickly.

If you are bent forward when you walk, you are halfway to a fall. If you walk with a cane or walker, you should be especially vigilant if you are slouched over while walking. I would like to thank my physical trainer, Mr. Tom Hijack, for teaching me how to stand and walk properly without falling down.

He said to imagine you have a hook comfortably and lovingly attached to your collarbone. It is attached to an unbreakable string that reaches up to the ceiling or the sky. It holds you up, provides balance and gives you perfect posture. Wherever you go, always hold yourself up by your hook. You will feel better, look better, and will walk with confidence. Doing so greatly helps alleviate back pain. When you use this hook, you can easily achieve spinal alignment and your back can be at peace, with each vertebra perfectly lined up, one on top of another.

Antidepressants/Anxiety Medication
Costada

Many intelligent people go to see a psychiatrist if they are feeling depressed or anxious. If they find themselves in a state of constant worry, sad, overwhelmed, not being able to sleep or worse, their doctor may put them on antidepressants or anxiety medication to help control these types of feelings. Throughout this book the spirit guides offer ways for us to achieve happiness. One way is to take antidepressants if needed. When we asked Costada what she thought of people taking antidepressants, she said no two babies are alike. Some may have their internal chemistry out of balance. It's not that it's bad, it's just off. When this is the case, they sometimes need to take medication that will provide what is lacking in their blood, thereby healing them.

There are other treatments for depression and anxiety, but because everybody is different, some people need antidepressants to put their mind into a natural state. Costada recommends taking them only if they make you feel better. There is nothing wrong with taking a pill if your body needs it. If a person is depressed but doesn't know if they should take the next step and consider medication, they should ask their guides if they can have a better life if they go on an antidepressant. In general, the guides don't like medication, although they do say that at times it is beneficial and even necessary. Furthermore, you don't have to stay on it forever.

Some people have problems with taking pills. They believe it makes them appear weak or that it represents there is something wrong with them. Costada says this is foolish. The medication is a way to simply correct our body chemistry. There's nothing weak about taking a pill. According to the guides, people who are critical of taking medication are keeping something that's good for them out of their reach. It's like when someone throws you a life preserver, but you don't reach for it. It's a sign of strength to know that you need something, and you should love yourself enough to do something about it and attain the chemical balance that you need to be happy.

People can tell that they are on the right medication because they should feel better within a few weeks. It's best to talk to your prescribing doctor about the effectiveness of the medication. Some people need to try more than one medication before finding the one that clicks.

Arcturians

The Arcturians recommend anxiety medication and say it is very good for you because the body shouldn't stay anxious. It's a very harsh state for the body to be in. Medication can be combined with other treatment methods for anxiety. Hypnotic regressions can help people overcome their anxiety. According to the Arcturians, this is because most anxiety is a holdover from a traumatic event earlier in our life or in a past life.

If someone is afraid to try an anxiety medication, the Arcturians urge these types of people to just try it for a few months. They don't have to think of it as a lifelong commitment. Again, talk to your doctor, try a pill and see if it helps. In addition, the guides say that as people get older, their anxiety tends to fade. That is because they just learn through the course of their life that there is not that much to be anxious about. There are few elderly people who are still as anxious as they were when they were young.

Unfortunately, depression does tend to affect the elderly. This might be because their friends die and they live a more solitary existence. As we age, we tend to worry about death (even though this is needless worry because we all have an eternal soul).

While medicine can help eliminate the effects of depression and anxiety if there is a chemical imbalance, the Arcturians say that at times antidepressants and anxiety medication cannot permanently rectify the problem. One can get rid of the underlying negative emotion by getting to the root of the problem. People need to find out what they're afraid of and determine what's making them anxious or depressed.

If it is not a chemical imbalance, the pills may not have a meaningful effect. At times it is just related to something traumatic that happened in one's past that the person cannot get over. In that case, the pills might help a little bit, but alternatively, it is possible that therapy could lead them into happiness. People should talk to someone, like a doctor, or a group of people experiencing the same type of feelings. Hypnotic therapy may be the answer. People can go into trance, talk to their spirit guide, and ask about the reason for their depression and anxiety. They can question what it relates to and what can be done to eliminate the underlying cause.

After being in trance, the Arcturians recommend that we write down in our journal what messages we received in trance. It will help in the future because you can read about past times you were depressed and what caused the depression to lift, reassuring you that your current depression is not permanent. Also, writing down your negative issues is good therapy, as well as keeping a gratitude journal.

The following meditation on healing is provided by hypnotherapist, Ms. Heather Zicko. However, if you have been doing the meditations all along, the body scans should have helped already with some problems. That is assuming you listened to the messages from your body and followed through on the requests. The follow-through is the key. (With the assistance of Ms. Zicko, I myself, using body scans, meditation, and traditional medicine, have healed miraculously from a vast number of illness including two terminal cancers and multiple sclerosis.)

Meditation Exercise for Self-Healing by Ms. Heather Zicko

Chapter 30
Weight and Self-Punishment

"Twist the optimist and the pessimist
the difference is droll:
the optimist sees the doughnut
but the pessimist sees the hole."
—Mc Landburgh Wilson

Humans have a strange habit of punishing themselves, particularly when it comes to our relationship with food. We can eat too much or not enough to try to get even with ourselves. Yet there is no logic to such action. Let your body and your hunger be your guide to eating. Be aware that some may find pleasure in eating. However, this might lead to overeating, which can harm your body. Other people must encourage themselves to eat because they know their energy level falls without food. Ask your guide to tell you what your natural weight is and be happy being that weight.

Costada

A person's weight is not important. What we do, how we feel and how we grow are important. Most of the animals alive are thin and don't have enough food. Unless they have just eaten, they are hungry, and they don't know where their next meal will come from. Meanwhile, people who have sufficient food might worry about their weight. Costada says this is not meaningful. There are so many more important things. We have to eat to live. It shouldn't mean anything more to us than that.

Some people focus too much on food and miss out on other activities in life. For some, eating is an easy solution to make them feel better. If one is getting proper nourishment through food and savoring it at the same time, feeling better is a good outcome. If someone is overeating or undereating because they are unhappy, they're punishing themselves. So, some people either eat too much – more than our body wants or needs – or they keep themselves from eating enough when their bodies actually need more. There should be a happy medium that is the correct way to love and take care of our bodies.

Among the animals on earth, Costada notes that only humans punish themselves with food. Humans represent the only species that has problems with food. All other animals know how important food is. They don't overeat to punish themselves.

The top three things we can learn from animals about eating include:

1. Food is fuel, and we need it to live. Once we have enough, we can go about our business and just have fun.

2. We should have food stored up for when we're hungry.

3. Our bodies know when we need to eat. The key is to listen to our bodies rather than our minds telling us "it's time to eat". We only need to eat when our stomach tells us to.

Overeating causes the body to work overtime and it takes too much energy to digest all of it. We also can't use our bodies properly if they're big and fat. It's difficult to move, and we may not like the way we feel or look. These things make us unhappy, even if they are not that important overall. Overeating can restrict our movement. Or, if we don't eat enough, we don't have energy to get out of bed. We are easily fatigued. Both situations can lead to sad, unhappy lives. At the extreme, it causes us to live the life of a shut-in. It's the ultimate punishment. We've put ourselves in jail.

Arcturians

Punishing ourselves with food is an activity the Arcturians don't understand. In their view, there is no need for this. In terms of losing or gaining weight, they don't see the difference 10 or 20 pounds one way or the other makes. Yet as humans, we set out all sorts of objectives for ourselves, but they are unnecessary. If we can't accomplish these often unrealistic goals, we feel bad – we've failed. To lessen our frustration, we might seek solace in food. Something that tastes good might take our mind off our bad feelings. We might find that the simplest thing to do is to eat – or not eat at all. Though we might think this will lessen the hurt, neither of these things do anything to help us reach happiness or prosperity. Punishing ourselves and our bodies needlessly is one of our biggest problems. Weight issues can signify that you've moved too far from nature and your life path and are therefore out of balance.

Arcturians say we can regain our balance, but we first must find what is making us punish ourselves with food. Is it something about ourselves that we don't like and want to change but can't? Or is it a stressful situation that makes us want "comfort food"? Any number of things can trigger bad eating habits. Food is necessary for life so either overeating or undereating is pointless as the result is simply harm to our bodies. The guides say overeating and undereating are completely related – simply different sides of a coin.

People who are happy and centered don't focus on food. When their body is hungry, they eat. When their body is satisfied, they stop. Too many people let their minds override their bodies' needs and wants. The Arcturians say the solution is to bring in more pleasure. When we're happy and engaged, we don't eat out of proportion. If we're dancing and having a good time with friends, we're not thinking about harming ourselves.

Rely on your self-love, the love of your guides and the love of others. If you have shut yourself off from friends, make a concerted effort to open yourself up to others. Imagine being with friends and not alone. Imagine doing something other than seeking comfort with or without food.

The Arcturians say that some people just don't think they deserve to be happy. They say this is one of our biggest failings as humans. The problem is widespread. Some people deal with unhappiness by getting angry at themselves. The Arcturians explain that we learn when we're young that if we do something bad, we get punished. This can unfortunately lead to adults punishing themselves with food or by other means.

John

John says he doesn't punish himself with food and the other birds don't either. We should be as smart as they are.

Katrina Blecher

Meditation Exercise for Weight Management

Chapter 31
Prosperity

"When the One Great Scorer comes to write against your
name –
He marks – not that you won or lost – but how you play the
game."

—Grantland Rice

Unless you love numbers and finance, you might find this chapter dull. Sorry. People usually equate prosperity with dollars. Though not incorrect, we are also prosperous in other ways, including love, health, wisdom and happiness. Money is a very small part of prosperity. The angels define true prosperity as being happy with having enough of what we need. More than that is unnecessary. The ultimate sense of prosperity is enlightenment, when you realize you have all you desire. The angels suggest keeping a record of how much money we make and spend. This could be updated monthly, but only if it's something you want to do. There is no need to complicate your life, as great record keeping doesn't impact one's wealth.

Costada

Costada says that we have a tendency to confuse abundance with prosperity. Abundance is when we have too much so there's going to be waste. Prosperity is just perfect. It is similar to gratitude, as gratitude is feeling happy with what the world gives you. She also states that we are all prosperous because we are free to go after whatever we want or do whatever we want. We have the freedom to be happy with what we have and to be excited about what we desire.

From a practical standpoint, the first step to prosperity is positive cash flow. In the exercise at the end of the chapter, tables are provided to help you get your finances in order. The first line in the table is income, which is your take home pay plus income from other sources, such as investments. Then, list all of your monthly expenses. If your expenses total more than your income, you are either building up credit card debt, borrowing money or not paying bills. This situation can not last.

The angels say that there are all these dollars floating around. You can't easily change how many you get, but you can change how many you spend or give away. If you spend a little less per month than you make, you will have positive cash flow. You should have the extra money automatically taken out of your checking account and put it into some form of savings. If you adjust your expenses and are saving a little every month, know that you've succeeded and don't need to worry about money. Don't forget about manifestation. You can manifest your desires. It is also how you can increase your wealth.

Arcturians

The Arcturians say that in order to get your finances under control, it is important to look at what you own; in other words, know your assets. You want to take really good care of your assets and help them grow. Your assets are all the positive and tangible things you have in your life, such as your home, car, investments, belongings, everything you own. Write down all your assets and how much each is worth. When you know how much you have, you will probably be surprised. You should remember this feeling every time you are about to buy something new. That way you will know you already have enough and want less. That's why you should keep things clean, light and open so you can see and appreciate your assets.

The wonderful thing about assets is that time is on their side. Over time, they naturally become more valuable due to inflation. You just have to maintain them, they'll grow on their own. Obtaining more assets is not a meaningful goal. Rather, just keep the assets you own in good condition. The guides say that people don't need more. We just need to appreciate what we already own. The ultimate is to save a little each month. Find the pleasure in opening up a bill and seeing a small balance due, and even more pleasure to be found as your saving balance rises. Find displeasure in buying nonessential items as they just take away from your savings.

Once you have enough saved up, you might want to invest in the stock market. Over time, it has been shown that the best return for an individual investor is to buy a no-load (no commission) S&P 500 Index fund. Over time, on average the S&P 500 has outperformed approximately 85% - 90% of all other mutual funds. This is for your stock investments. You also need to have some bonds, or fixed income investments. The younger you are, the more you should have in stocks, increasing the percentage of fixed income as you age. A rule of thumb is fixed income should equal your age. If you are 20, then 20% of you money should be in bond funds. If you are 80, then 80% of your money should be in bond funds. The safer bond funds are investment grade. It's recommended that one-third should be in a short-term investment grade bond fund, one-third in intermediate term and one-third in a long-term bond fund. This should also be a no commission product. For example, Vanguard is the largest no commission brokerage firm and has a good reputation.

John

We think prosperity has to do with material objects, but humans are the only ones who think this way. Animals are more invested in food. John feels a little put out because he needs to talk about liabilities and he thinks they are "yucky." Liabilities are everything you owe. The guides don't like that, and John says we should put all our efforts into getting rid of them. Every time you reduce or get rid of a liability, you become that much richer.

John says that you should first pay off people to whom you owe money. Borrowing money can be harmful to relationships. Next, you should pay off your credit card bills because they tend to have the highest rate of interest. Remember, not to charge more than you can pay back each month. Once you pay off your credit cards, try to stop the shopping that builds debt back up. Find the joy in saving. Lastly, don't forget all the money you spent in the past on items you did not need; think how much happier you would be today if that money was in the bank.

Once you list all your assets and liabilities (debt) you have made a balance sheet. Take the assets you own and subtract all you owe. If it's a positive number, congratulations. You are financially prosperous. You have a positive net worth (or equity, which is the difference between assets and liabilities so the balance sheet balances). The amount of equity you have is equal to your monetary worth. However, this is not what you are worth as a soul, which is obviously so much more. If it is a negative number and you owe a lot of money, you need to have a long-term plan on how you are going to pay what you owe. It may take a couple of years, but the best way to accomplish this is to spend less.

Lastly, John sent three birds, each with a message about prosperity. The first bird said that he is prosperous because he was enlightened and cherishes everything he has. The second bird stated that prosperity is like music. It's all around us. We should remove the blinders that prevent us from believing that we don't have what we need. The final bird squawked that we are able to do whatever we want whenever we want. It's this type of freedom that makes us prosperous.

The above financial advice is simple but sound. It is similar to the medical advice given to improve health: watch your diet, exercise and don't smoke.

Exercise for Getting Finances in Order
Monthly Income Statement
Income:
After-tax salary $
Other income

Total Income $

Expenses:

Housing (including property taxes) $

Insurance

Food

Home maintenance/repairs

Utilities & fuel

Telephone/cable/internet

Transportation/auto expense

Clothing

Dry cleaning/laundry

Health Club

Hairdresser, etc.

Domestic Help

Entertainment

Travel/vacations

Doctors/medication

Gifts/contributions

Other

Total Expenses $

Net Income or Cash Flow (Income less expenses) $

Goal: Have this be a positive number, i.e., positive cash flow.

Balance Sheet/Net Worth Statement

Assets:

Bank accounts $

Real estate

Investments

Auto

Furniture & household Accessories

Other

Total Assets $

Liabilities and Net Worth:

Credit card balances $

Mortgage

Car loan

Other loans (debt)

Total Liabilities $

Net worth or equity (Assets minus liabilities) $

Goal: Have this also be a positive number.

Chapter 32
From Anxiety to Rebirth

"Yet they, believe me, who await
No gifts from Chance, have conquered Fate."
—Matthew Arnold

Every day we awaken is a fresh day. Unfortunately, some thoughts and emotions tend to linger from the day before, like anxiety. We have the ability to get to the basis of why we are anxious. Having the knowledge that we can eliminate anxiety and change our life at any moment can be life altering. Once our anxiety is understood and overcome, it is comparable to being reborn.

Costada

One time while I was in trance, Costada appeared wearing a light pink gown. She normally wears white robes. She says the pink represented spring, new growth, and rebirth. She says everyone can be reborn every day. We can make our life exactly as we choose. We don't have to carry over any baggage from the day before. This can be tricky, as some emotions like to hang around like bad cooking odors. Anxiety is one of the most difficult to dispose of.

Costada explained that anxiety is worrying to the point of suffering about an imaginary event that many occur in your future. She says unwarranted anxiety is usually the result of a childhood trauma. Not everyone had a great childhood. Something, she said, may have made us anxious many years ago and we haven't calmed down yet. Or it could be a holdover from a past life event. Anxiety is not having the faith and trust that everything will work out fine.

A permanent resolution to anxiety can be achieved in trance by getting to the root cause. However, a short-term fix to anxiety can be found in breathing. If you find yourself nervous and you are not in danger, you're probably experiencing anxiety. To calm your mind, get into a comfortable position and close your eyes. Inhale, and feel your abdomen expand. Exhale and notice how your belly sinks down. Every time you exhale, say to yourself, "deep sleep." Focus on your breathing and the feel of your stomach while you take 12 breaths. At the end, slowly open your eyes, pat yourself gently for the good work. Continue on with your day, actively avoiding any thoughts about the topic that made you anxious.

Here is a good technique for starting a new day. Realize you have woken up to a fresh day with no need to carry over issues from the past. Instead, upon awakening we should say a positive affirmation such as, "today I will feel joy." You can substitute alternatives such as happiness or bliss or any other positive emotion. She also suggests that upon awakening, but still in bed, we should imagine it's the first day of spring and we can do anything we want. Even your body has been reborn overnight. Every day we should start with our dreams. If we focus on them, we can turn them into reality. Everything in the past should be let go except for good relationships and happy memories. People need encouragement to live their dreams. First, we have to know it is possible. Choose to let your heart decide, and then live them moment by moment.

Costada offers the following technique on listening to the positive emotions from our heart, instead of the anxious thoughts in our head: We can't have the life of our dreams if we don't know what they are, and they can't be the dreams of yesterday. We have to decide what we want each day, without planning in advance. Just know it's a new day and you can enjoy every moment. Every day can improve. Following your dreams is how you find your right life path, which makes your life fantastic. Following your dreams takes you further away from the cause of your anxiety.

1. We should ask ourselves three questions every morning: What do I want to do today? (Not, what do I have to do today?)

2. Will it make me happy?

3. If the answer is yes, take a moment of gratitude to think about how fortunate you are to be able to do something with this day that makes you happy.

4. If the answer is no (for example, if you have to go to work and you don't feel like it) identify one thing you can do for yourself today that will make you feel good. Perhaps it's stopping for a fresh juice on your way to work or making a plan to watch your new favorite TV show when you get home.

Arcturians

When discussing anxiety, the Arcturians point to butterflies. That is because they can represent the nervous feeling of butterflies in your stomach. They also represent metamorphosis by changing from a caterpillar to a beautiful flying creature. When we put our anxiety into its appropriate level of importance, the Arcturians say we will be transformed and reborn.

The Arcturians believe that there is always a reason for having anxiety and that this feeling will leave on its own as soon as you discover and relive the event that caused it. When you relive it, the experience will be in the forefront of your conscious. You will, however, realize that the event happened in the past. Also, you will be clearheaded when you analyze the likelihood of it happening to you again. Then you can make a plan of what you would do if it did happen again.

Once a fear is known, it ceases to reside in the background, causing you to be uneasy. The more you get to know exactly what you fear, the more you can root around in it, pull it apart and study it. The relief and calm you feel as you explore it will amaze you. Be assured, if you are never able to determine exactly what you are afraid of or why, anxiety naturally fades as we age.

According to the Arcturians, our biggest fear is death. However, after doing a past life regression you will know that you have lived before and so you will live again after you die. This knowledge will alleviate most of your anxiety. It will no longer be a part of you. This will allow you to grow up and be a self-confident adult. Just leave the nervousness in your past. You can be reborn into a new whole, self-assured person, like you're meant to be.

They also give advice on following our dreams, saying that dreams are the reason we are here. Following them will lead us away from our fears. We came to earth with a purpose and our life is better when we know what that purpose is and move towards it. If we don't know what our purpose is or what our dreams are, we have to force ourselves to start to dream. The Arcturians say it's not difficult because everyone has an idea of what they want. The last message from the Arcturians is: do not forget that before birth, there is light.

The Arcturians offer the following exercise to help live your dreams. Imagine yourself as a perfect little baby and know that you still have that little baby inside of yourself. This demonstrates that you are just as healthy and loved today as you were as a baby before some event caused you to be frequently anxious. Your job is to love this baby and take care of it. Completely relive what caused your anxiety, explore the event from a safe distance and allow yourself to grow up again without it having any impact on you.

Meditation Exercise for Releasing Anxiety

Before you begin the meditation, try to think of a fear you want to address that is neither logical nor in proportion to real danger. In the meditation, you will do another regression. This time to a childhood or a past life event responsible for the fear. At the end of the meditation, see how this event relates to your current fear and how likely is it to happen again.

Chapter 33
Music

"When I am silent, I fall into the place where everything is
music."

—Rumi

*They call me Kate. Yet my real name, like everyone's soul name, is
actually a beautiful melody. When the Lord created us, he gave us
our own musical names. The stunning music that you can hear
when you are in a deep trance is the music of your true name. This
amazing music is coming from you. There is almost an infinite
number of souls, and luckily there exists an infinite amount of
melodies. This is one reason the guides say that music is a very
integral part of our being.*

Costada

In order to hear the sound of your soul, Costada suggests
going into trance and imagining that you are outside on a lovely
meadow or hillside. You are alone with your guides. Listen to the
silence. Off in the distance, you hear something. Keep listening
until you can make it out. What do you hear? It may just be
one note or many. Costada says these sounds are the sounds in
the air. The more you listen, the more you hear. She stresses that
everything is surrounded by beautiful sounds.

She notes that in a trance it is important to focus on the music and try to feel the sound waves or vibrations (this will resonate best for those who have a strong auditory sense). Notice the sounds hitting and entering not just your eardrums, but your entire being. Feel the waves of sound. They are in the exact vibration as the cells in your body.

There is always sound. It radiates from every living soul. As a result, everything is constantly vibrating and moving. Costada says that if you look at a cell under a microscope, you can see the inside parts of the cell moving. They are moving in sync with the music, gently swaying. In the same manner, all of our organs and muscles and insides slide together so easily within our bodies because of this beautiful music. Sound can be likened to the oil between the parts of a clock mechanism; it allows the parts to mesh together smoothly so the timepiece works perfectly. We are not just moving to the music; we are the music.

Costada believes that the music is everywhere and we should take the time to listen to it. She describes music as the most beautiful of sounds. You first hear the beauty of silence and then hear musical notes floating in the air like those made by wind chimes. Imagine the notes as all different pastel colors. The message of the music and colors is that sound is power, just limitless power floating in the air. We can have as much as we want. Drink in the beauty of the sounds, so you feel like you have a silken sheet of musical notes lightly covering you.

Arcturians

Arcturians say that music focuses everything in our body on the correct rhythm, so that the body functions perfectly and is in the proper vibration. Everything within us needs to move. It needs to move to the music of our souls.

They say the musicality of our names comes from God. Our parents gave us the name we use in this life, but when our soul came into existence, it came in as light, love, courage and music. Each soul is unique, and its music is equally unique.

Everybody knows each other by their sound. This is why, they explain, the whole air sings. It is the reason that everything is light because we are beings of light. In lives between lives, where we spend most of our time, there is simply light, music and love. The Arcturians say that the deaf can hear the music and the blind can see the light when they do meditative regressions to the period of lives between lives.

When a person is not moving to the music or is out of sync with the music, they can become ill or unhappy. The Arcturians attribute this to the degree of effort exerted when people are fighting their natural rhythm. They are not listening to the music. Put another way, they are not listening to their instincts. It is enjoyable to listen to the inside silence until we can hear the wondrous music of our souls.

When someone is unhappy or emotionally ill, they should play music on the outside. Play anything you want to listen to at that moment. Just move and, if you are able, let yourself dance to it. Your body will absorb the sounds and the vibrations. Imagine the sound flowing through you. You will happily be brought back into the moment.

They say music can really change our mood. For instance, sometimes people put on music that makes them sad. Doing this is not advisable because it isn't good for the body. The happy vibration of your soul clashes with the music that makes you sad. If it makes you happy and increases your vibrational level, then that is the music for you.

Don't forget to listen to the silence. You can hear so much: your breathing, a breeze, and small, previously unnoticed sounds. There is so much we never listen to, such beauty we are missing. The Arcturians say there are not different kinds of music, there is only music.

John

He soars on musical notes. The air is full of them and it keeps him above the ground. That's why birds squawk and chirp, because the music builds up and they can't hold it inside. That's what we should be doing – whistling and singing – that's true happiness.

He says that music, movement, light, and color are constant. They are always there and are part of us. We see and appreciate colors and shapes, but we tend to ignore sound, and it's just as important. Your soul name is harmony and sounds beautiful. It flows through you and everything vibrates so happily. We're drawn to music because it starts within us. Our soul just wants to be heard.

If we don't have music, we have a large hole in our lives and we can feel empty. However, there's no need because the music is always there. He says the music starts in our mother's womb, in this life. It's like the ocean and the waves coming to the shore. The movement and sound are constant – you can count on it.

Ron NaVarre – Stress Defense

Hearing your soul name is not easy. Therefore, I enlisted the help of my associate Mr. Ron NaVarre. He helped me hear my soul's name. He has graciously recorded the meditation for this chapter.

Meditation for Hearing Your Soul's Musical Name by Mr. Ron NaVarre

Chapter 34
Love – Self-love

"Let those love now who never loved before;
let those who always loved, now love the more."
—Thomas Parnell

Love is the strongest feeling you will get from your angel. When you experience the overwhelming love of your angel, you will love them in return. It will happen naturally. You respect them so much that you acknowledge that if they, these perfect souls, can love you so intensely you must certainly deserve their love. You cannot disagree with them, so you cannot fail to love yourself. You will experience absolute self-love. When you have self-love, you are golden.

Arcturians

Arcturians say that self-love is really going to change everyone's life. We have to realize how much love we are continually receiving from our spirit guides and the Lord.

According to the Arcturians, love doesn't just come from the people in your life, as many assume. Rather it comes from God, the angels, your soul, other animals, and the earth itself. It's limiting to feel we want more evidence of love from other people. Other people's love is just a small part of all the love that is out there.

We can never have too much love. It is always being replenished just as we are always giving it out. It stays in balance, even if we are not aware of it. Although we are so full of love, there are often times when we forget, and we can't feel it. When this happens, the Arcturians say we are not feeling worthy. It reflects a time when we did not receive a sufficient amount of self-love. This is the time to meditate and ask your guide for help in finding out why you have these feelings of unworthiness. The Arcturians say it is important to know that you are indeed worthy of love. You should realize that you are just blocking yourself from understanding this.

Love is an adventure, and the Arcturians want us to experience new ideas through adventure. They suggest taking small or short journeys that will lead to finding love in unexpected places, perhaps, for example, the love you feel for a simple cornflower in a bright green field. Go somewhere new and find what is waiting for you. The Arcturians believe that there is always something wonderful waiting for us to discover.

Consider it a goal to have loving relationships that allow you to become remarkably close to other people. In terms of love between couples, you will grow, learn and become happier because of the love you share. See how this love lets both of you flourish. If one is at a loss about how to improve the love in a relationship, go into a trance and call in the other person. Ask your guide what the other person's guide has to say that will make the other person happy. Then make it happen.

Costada

Self-love is the greatest gift the angels give us. Although the love emanates from ourselves, the guides are instrumental in helping us bring our love to the forefront, as they allow us to genuinely think about ourselves and what we deserve. Nothing will have a greater impact in our life. Once we have total self-love, we will find it easy to love others. We will feel connected to all living creatures, as well as the earth and sky.

Costada notes that the better we take care of ourselves and treat ourselves in a correct and loving manner, the more self-love we have. No one can take care of us better than we can. But the angels can give us help in that direction. It takes practice to indulge ourselves at times and think about our own happiness and prosperity, but the more we do, the more fulfilling life will become.

Love is not something to be stockpiled. It should be shared. As much as you give out, you get just as much back. Just like breathing. Sometimes she admits that we may not feel like we are getting enough love. She explains that this is merely our current perception. In truth, she says, we have endless love around us, but at times we set up barriers so we can't accept love. She recommends asking your guide:

1. Why have I cut myself off from love?
2. What is the purpose of the barriers I have put up?
3. How do those barriers serve me?
4. Do I want to eliminate them?

5. If you are ready to remove those barriers, ask your angel for a specific exercise or phrase to repeat in order to release the barriers with love.

6. If you are not yet ready, be kind with yourself and know that you deserve to accept love and that one day you shall. You angel will guide you down the path once the question is asked.

John

I am love, no doubt about it. Love is who we are.

Meditation Exercise to Realize Self-Love

Chapter 35
Enlightenment

"For man, as for flower and beast and bird, the supreme triumph is to be most vividly most perfectly alive."
—David Lawrence

Enlightenment is the ultimate. It is being as much like the person God wants us to be as we can. Enlightenment is not something you find, but rather something you realize. You realize it is there, has always been there and will remain forever. It is the realization that everything is great in your world. You don't need to be enlightened to have a great life, it's just hard to have a bad life if you're enlightened.

Costada

According to Costada, enlightenment is perfection. It's when we know everything around us is alive and sparkling, and it's never going to dim or go away. You will know you're enlightened because you're so happy, at peace with the world, in love with yourself and all of life. You feel connected and secure. Everything around you will thrive, and you'll know there is nothing bad. You'll experience all the high vibrational emotions and none of the negative ones. You'll know all your dreams are within your reach.

Costada says if we want to start down the path of enlightenment, we should start working on it and know it will happen. It may take years, but it will be a wonderful experience and we are meant to enjoy each moment of it. Costada says that we can identify those who are enlightened because they are a joy to be with, are helpful and seem to always have a wonderful answer to our questions. Enlightened people lift you up by making you feel better about yourself. There's nothing difficult about them, they're all light energy. They are the people everyone gravitates toward.

She compares enlightenment to a curtain. When we walk through it, everything is wonderful. We simply see all the beauty and none of the negatives - our eyes just pass over them. We only see the goodness, and then life flows effortlessly.

Take a look at the path behind you. All the flowers are sprouting up and all the negatives are burying themselves into the earth and fading away.

One day, we'll realize we have no more curtains and that everything negative has gone away. It's so beautiful. We are then forever happy, calm, and full of love for all living souls. We know we're on this wonderful journey forever. We are enlightened.

Arcturians

Arcturians say that when we realize we are enlightened, our whole life changes. It will let our soul free. It practically never goes away. Or if it does briefly, it's a snap to have it again.

In order to realize enlightenment, the negatives must be peeled away. Get rid of all of it through acceptance. Go through each negative emotion, figure out the cause and decide whether it should be kept or thrown away. If we keep it, we have to accept it with love, so it ceases to have any negative impact upon us. With enlightenment we will experience a depth of knowledge and insight that will forever change us and we will never forget.

The Arcturians say that only 1%-2% of the people on the planet are enlightened right now. Naturally, all spirit guides are enlightened. They say you will know if you are enlightened because everything is perfect, everything glows, and you have all your answers. You just see beauty. You just want to do good things and help others.

The Arcturians explain the difference between enlightenment and spirituality. Spirituality is the sum of our thoughts and beliefs. Enlightenment is insight into how we feel and exist. It's much deeper. When you're enlightened, all your beliefs in spirituality simply become facts to you.

Children are born enlightened, but then they lose it. The Arcturians say it's usually something that people find in the second half of their lives. More people do not find enlightenment because they are too busy fighting day-to-day battles and they miss the big picture. They deny themselves all the beauty life has to offer. The Arcturians suggest we dispose of all our obsessive thoughts about little things. Enlightenment is clarity of what is profoundly important.

Animals experience enlightenment but not in the same manner as adults. Animals do not have all the negativity that most people do. So, they're almost enlightened naturally, even though their lives are harder than ours. For example, they don't have heat in the winter and don't know where their next meal is coming from. For people, it is easier because we're the most advanced animals. When we are enlightened, we realize the search is over, and we are here to simply relax and enjoy. To learn and to teach.

John

John describes enlightenment as perfection. It is flying up in the beautiful sky. It takes no effort, and it is an exuberant experience. Everything is so clear. We see things as they really are. They're really good.

He says nature is enlightened. It has no negatives. If we spend time in nature, it will teach us. Everything in nature moves so easily and smoothly, and that's what we're meant to do.

Not everyone becomes enlightened before they die, but we're all enlightened in lives between lives after we die. There are no shortcuts to realizing enlightenment, but it's a wonderful process so there's no reason to hurry through it. Life is the way to enlightenment.

Meditation Exercise for Enlightenment

Enlightenment requires little work on our part. It's already here. We only have to take away the barriers. This is not a recorded meditation. Rather, it is an outline for meditations to do on your own.

1. The angels recommend going into a trance.

2. Imagine walking through a field with magically suspended curtains all over.

3. As you approach, put out your hands, spread the curtains, and walk through them.

4. Each curtain represents a negative emotion which you walk through and put behind you.

5. The angels recommend doing at least one meditation per negative emotion. (Similar to the manner in which this book is laid out). Walk with a happy heart and release all negative feelings as you walk through the curtain. This will indicate you've healed yourself from the pain. You may occasionally need to revisit it and walk through the pain again, but it will lessen each time.

6. We must remember to be gentle with ourselves as we aim to resolve and accept each issue.

7. We need to walk through the fear and get it behind us.

8. Walk through the sadness.

9. When there is anxiety, self-doubt, grief, fear or worry, try to release these negative emotions and find lasting peace.

10. Inside us we have the courage to find forgiveness. When we need help, we always have our angels.

11. Leave the negative emotions on the path behind you until there's nothing left but light, love, joy, and knowledge.

Chapter 36
Conclusion

"Where there is charity and wisdom, there is neither fear nor
ignorance. Where there is patience and humility, there is
neither anger nor vexation. Where there is poverty and joy,
there is neither greed nor avarice. Where there is peace and
meditation, there is neither anxiety nor doubt."

—Saint Francis of Assisi

*Everybody has the power to be as prosperous and happy as they want.
When we are enlightened, we can't help but be elated. We have
immeasurable power and are capable of deep love. It is due to this
power that the fabric of our life can be as colorful and as textured
as we choose. Paint your life with the realization of your dreams
and effortlessly soar.*

Costada

This book should end, according to Costada, with highlights
from the guides. She says to remember that everything flows
easily and endlessly. The key is to just flow through life, knowing
that life continues on. We should take joy in that. She said that
when you find happiness, life moves smoothly and naturally,
and it never stops.

We cannot look for prosperity and happiness or wait for it to find us. Happiness is just within us, but at times it is buried deep within so we have to work hard to let the happiness come out and shine a light on our path in life. So, when we look inward and find our happiness, we know that if we lose it, we'll always be able to find it again. Prosperity is the realization that you have everything you need to be happy and healthy.

Costada says the guides have provided exceptional information which is recorded in this book and we should refer back to the areas that call to us. There are messages for everybody, waiting to be found.

She states that all the information in this book is solid and provides the steps necessary to happiness and prosperity. If you just walk down that path, you'll come to a beautiful place and it will surround you and consume you. Once you've found this intense happiness, nothing can ever take it away. Like the elements of the earth, it will never be destroyed. You've found your correct path and are enlightened.

Arcturians

Arcturians believe everything in the book is true, but if people don't believe it, that's fine with them. The spirit guides are always with us, love us and protect us. However, the Arcturians emphasize that everyone would be much happier if they talked to their guides because the guides hold all the answers to all our questions.

They suggest that the summary should include the highlights of the book to just remind us of what we should do on our journey to happiness and prosperity.

1. The first thing we should do is meet our angels.

2. Realize that we are eternal beings and can communicate with all eternal beings.

3. Acknowledge that all is perception. Realize you have control over your thoughts and actions.

4. Engage in activities that make your spirit soar.

5. Be kind to all living things.

6. Look for magic within every day.

7. We should love our bodies and our souls completely.

John

All the people who read this book will be happy and prosperous and will eventually fly off together to a magical place. We can teach others all we learned about attaining happiness and prosperity. This journey to prosperity and happiness will spread out before us as wide as the Amazon rainforest and as tall as Mt. Everest. John also is keen on enlightenment for everyone. He supports the premise that everyone should meet and talk to their spirit guides. He wants everyone to know that as souls, they will be able to fly around the cosmos as he does during lives between lives. He believes that happiness can be achieved if you follow your correct path and use the information in this book to help you on your journey. That said, if anyone doesn't take the information in the book seriously, he says he just might just swoop down and nibble on their toes.

About the Author

Kate Blecher holds a degree in economics from Barnard College, Columbia University and was certified as a professional hypnotherapist in 2013. She began a career on Wall Street as a securities analyst. Throughout her career, Kate was among the top financial services analysts in the country and was named a Wall Street Journal All-Star Analyst.

While Kate adored the work, the long hours and constant travel took a toll on her physical body, wherein she entered her second career as a professional patient. She excelled in this field as well, picking up well over 50 medical titles (diseases/conditions). Working with her guides and other master healers, Kate further expanded and honed her healing skills, which helped her survive four terminal conditions. In 2013, Kate founded Kate's Holistic Healing, Inc. As a hypnotherapist, she teaches clients to use their own bodies' natural power to heal. She is the author of books on self-healing and meditation. She lives in New York with her husband, Tony, and their cat.

www.ingramcontent.com/pod-product-compliance
Lightning Source LLC
Chambersburg PA
CBHW031502120626
46545CB00005B/1706